"Tara Beth Leach is woman who fell in love with Jesus as a teen and has only fallen deeper in love. As a pastor, she is a prophetic voice for God. In *Radiant Church* she deploys that voice, as only a prophet can, to call the church back to the heart of God. Tara Beth reminds us of who we are, how God sees us, and how we can be a more loving, thoughtful, a more gracious people in the world. She reminds us that the church is a unique beauty, a radiant beauty."

Sean Palmer, author of *Forty Days on Being a Three*, teaching pastor at Ecclesia Houston

"In her customarily personal and pastoral manner, Tara Beth provides a clear and compelling glimpse of the church Jesus loves so dearly. When the light seems to have grown dim, she helps us notice the radiance within and how we can be bearers of this radiant good news. If you're about to give up on the church, wait. Read this first. And don't be surprised if you begin to be drawn in by the beautiful and robust vision of Jesus' church for the first time, again."

J.R. Briggs, author of *The Sacred Overlap* and founder of Kairos Partnerships

"Radiance is not a common term for Christian theology, and it is often ignored in ecclesiology, but Tara Beth has rescued this term and made it central. The church is radiant—like a bride—when Jesus is central, when God's kingdom work forms a church, and when all its habits, practices, and virtues emerge from the Spirit who radiates the presence of Christ through each of us as we together embody the gospel about our radiant Lord. Here is a pastor who loves the church emoting her love for what Christ wants for the church."

Scot McKnight, author of *The Jesus Creed* and professor of New Testament at Northern Seminary

"Racism, sexism, and many other injustices plague our world and corrupt our Christian witness. Tara Beth Leach confronts this darkness with the transformative good news of Jesus Christ. She doesn't talk down to us; she walks with us in a journey from lament, to repentance, to radiant living. *Radiant Church* is for any individual or group looking to refine and rejuvenate their witness in a climate of love, grace, and kindness."

Douglas S. Bursch, pastor of Evergreen Church and author of *Posting Peace*

"In *Radiant Church*, Tara Beth Leach writes pastorally and prophetically about the state of the White evangelical church in America. This is a gutsy book. Leach beckons us to follow Jesus that we might become radiant, shining stars, alluring—no matter the cost. Easy, right? Wrong. In the US at least, it seems like Christians seeking to follow Jesus are often targeted and lampooned by other Christians. Even so, Leach encourages us to move forward through repentance and by allowing the light of Christ to radiate out from us. What makes this book especially strong is that Pastor Leach practices what she preaches. It's not mere talk. And therefore, it's exceedingly refreshing."

Marlena Graves, author of *The Way Up Is Down: Becoming Yourself by Forgetting Yourself*

"Tara Beth Leach believes in and deeply loves the church; she also knows that something has gone seriously wrong within much of the American church. In *Radiant Church* we find a prophetic critique of our various American idolatries, but one that avoids embittered cynicism. Throughout *Radiant Church*, the passion Tara Beth Leach has for Jesus Christ shines in every chapter. May this book help the American church return to its first love."

Brian Zahnd, founding pastor of Word of Life Church in St. Joseph, Missouri, and author of *Postcards from Babylon*

"The ability to simultaneously comfort and confront is rare, and this is exactly what Tara Beth Leach offers us in *Radiant Church*. With the evangelical church lingering at several cultural crossroads, many pastors and church leaders find themselves searching for a way forward. In our most honest moments, we find ourselves lacking conviction, fearful of a wrong step, and deeply anxious as we face an increasingly uncertain future."

Jay Y. Kim, pastor and author of *Analog Church*

"Pointing out the problems with the white evangelical church is easy. Showing the church how to draw on the abundant grace of God so we can live emboldened, empowered, and radiant lives, well, that's much more difficult. But that's exactly the task Tara Beth Leach sets for herself with this exuberant, thoughtful, and inspiring book. Written by a pastor who loves the church, *Radiant Church* is comforting and challenging in equal measure."

Michael Frost, author of *Surprise the World* and *The Shaping of Things to Come*

"Tara Beth Leach is one of the most radiant leaders I know! In the pages of *Radiant Church* she helps us properly lament issues of church life needing renovation. She then guides us forward to being a church in the radiant image of Jesus. I want to follow where she leads."

Todd Hunter, bishop, Churches for the Sake of Others, author of *Giving Church Another Chance*

"Like an experienced midwife, Tara Beth Leach leads us through the birth pangs of becoming the church that is to come. Not content to survive, she speaks words of encouragement to help a church flourish through these disruptive times. Anyone who has lived the tumultuous years of American church life these past few decades will find *Radiant Church* a calming wave of the Spirit preparing us all for the new day to come."

David Fitch, B. R. Lindner Chair of Evangelical Theology at Northern Seminary

"*Radiant Church* is a raw and unwavering look at the church as she is today, warts and all. Valiantly forthcoming and disarmingly real, Tara Beth Leach gives us the goods, showing us that despite our failures, Jesus is still here, calling us to radiance."

Bruxy Cavey, teaching pastor at The Meeting House and author of *The End of Religion*

"In *Radiant Church*, Tara Beth Leach does something radical: she looks to Jesus first, the light of the world in human flesh. Jesus calls us to know him and live like him in such a way that radical love should be what we are known for, not bigotry, hypocrisy, patriarchy, polarization, racism, political ideology, or any other negatively loaded label. Rather than watering down the Bible to make Christianity more palatable for our culture, she invites us to drink deeply of its story, to become people known for radiating God's beauty and goodness to our world. Read this prophetic book, and let's take up the abundant resources of Jesus together so we can put his vision of a *Radiant Church* on full display."

Kurt Willems, pastor, podcaster, and author of *Echoing Hope: How the Humanity of Jesus Redeems Our Pain*

"Tara Beth is a faithful and personable guide, bravely naming and unmasking some of the powers that have captivated white evangelicalism. We are captive to imitation, but there is only One who turns imitation into freedom and human flourishing. Tara Beth, through word and example, call us to imitate the Radiant One, so that we might live into our collective radiance and be billboards of New Creation."

JR Woodward, national director of The V3 Movement, author of *Creating a Missional Culture*, and coauthor of *The Church as Movement*

"Our friend Tara Beth nails it in *Radiant Church*. Something is deeply wrong in the prevailing understanding and experience of the contemporary evangelical church. We are called to a credible, indeed a radiant witness. But to get there, things need to change. Tara brings her compassionate and prophetic voice to bear in ushering in hope and possibility for the way forward. Well done!"

Alan and Deb Hirsch, authors and missional leaders, founders of Forge Mission Training Network

"*Radiant Church* is a brilliantly written challenge to become a church that beautifully reflects Jesus to a hurting and hopeless world. Tara Beth Leach smartly gives us a vision of a church that radiantly shines, while she also presents practical steps for becoming a pure and active people. I strongly encourage you to read *Radiant Church* and catch a glimpse of the church God meant us to be!"

Dave Ferguson, lead pastor of Community Christian Church, Naperville, Illinois, and author of *B.L.E.S.S.: 5 Everyday Ways to Love Your Neighbor and Change the World*

"Tara Beth loves the church enough to tell us the truth—the truth about our condition and our calling, the truth of God's mercy and of our mission. As a shepherd who has suffered blows both for the flock and from them, she writes with honesty and hope. Her theological insight and pastoral instincts are on display in this timely message for Christians and leaders today."

Glenn Packiam, associate senior pastor of New Life Church, Colorado Springs, and author of *Worship and the World to Come*

"*Radiant Church* exudes a love for Christ and the church through every page. The fruit is a biblical vision of the church, not located in large auditoriums or in the personhood of a charismatic leader, rather in what happens when the church seeks to be faithfully rooted in the right story. Through a clear and compelling look at how the evangelical church has largely failed in its witness, Tara brings forth a preview, along with practices and a prophetic witness, pointing to what happens when the church reclaims its true light. Indeed, if the church follows this repentant path, the world will behold the silhouette of Christ through a transformative witness."

José Humphreys, author of *Seeing Jesus in East Harlem*

"With piercing prophetic insight and a bold and crystal-clear voice, Tara Beth Leach calls out the many ways in which the church in America fundamentally conflicts with the radiant kingdom movement Jesus inaugurated. Yet as accurate and compelling as Tara Beth's critique of the church is, *Radiant Church* is one of the most inspired and hope-filled books I've ever read."

Greg Boyd, senior pastor, Woodland Hills Church, and author of *Cross Vision*

"*Radiant Church* pulls back the curtain ever so gently to expose our mission drift, but it doesn't stop there. Tara Beth Leach offers us illuminating and inviting ways to recover our light. Part manifesto, part vulnerable confession, this brilliant work is beckoning us to step forward into the blazing possibilities. Thank you, Tara Beth, for this brave gift to the community of Christ."

Dan White Jr., author of *Love Over Fear* and cofounder of the KINEO Center

"In case you've missed it, long-standing expressions of evangelicalism, those more reflective of the assumptions and characteristics of worldly power structures than the ways of Jesus and his kingdom, are being exposed and decried. This is difficult yet necessary work. It requires patience, discernment, and spiritual integrity on the part of church leaders. Tara Beth Leach is a wonderful example of such leadership, and *Radiant Church* is precisely the sort of book that helps us not only see and name the realities that have compromised our witness, but gives us a vision for a better, more faithful way forward."

JR Rozko, executive director, the Telos Collective

"I've had the privilege of being in the room when Tara Beth Leach talks about the church. She herself is radiant, not only describing but embodying the radiant beauty of the Bride of Christ. It makes us want to see what she sees and love what she loves. *Radiant Church* draws us into that vision, being honest about what is broken in the church, and at the same time lovingly reminding the weary church of her true character and mission."

Mandy Smith, pastor and author of *The Vulnerable Pastor* and *Unfettered*

RADIANT

CHURCH

RESTORING THE CREDIBILITY
OF OUR WITNESS

TARA BETH LEACH

An imprint of InterVarsity Press
Downers Grove, Illinois

InterVarsity Press
P.O. Box 1400, Downers Grove, IL 60515-1426
ivpress.com
email@ivpress.com

InterVarsity Press® is the book-publishing division of InterVarsity Christian Fellowship/USA®,
a movement of students and faculty active on campus at hundreds of universities, colleges, and schools
of nursing in the United States of America, and a member movement of the International Fellowship of
Evangelical Students. For information about local and regional activities, visit intervarsity.org.

All Scripture quotations, unless otherwise indicated, are taken from The Holy Bible, New International
Version®, NIV®. Copyright © 1973, 1978, 1984, 2011 by Biblica, Inc.™ Used by permission of Zondervan.
All rights reserved worldwide. www.zondervan.com. The "NIV" and "New International Version" are
trademarks registered in the United States Patent and Trademark Office by Biblica, Inc.™

While any stories in this book are true, some names and identifying information may have been changed
to protect the privacy of individuals.

Cover design and image composite: David Fassett
Interior design: Daniel van Loon
Images: abstract black rays: © rashpil / iStock / Getty Images Plus
        speed lines illustration: © inides / iStock / Getty Images Plus

ISBN 978-0-8308-4762-4 (print)
ISBN 978-0-8308-4763-1 (digital)

Printed in the United States of America ♾

InterVarsity Press is committed to ecological stewardship and to the conservation of natural resources
in all our operations. This book was printed using sustainably sourced paper.

Library of Congress Cataloging-in-Publication Data
A catalog record for this book is available from the Library of Congress.

P 25 24 23 22 21 20 19 18 17 16 15 14 13 12 11 10 9 8 7 6 5 4 3 2 1
Y 37 36 35 34 33 32 31 30 29 28 27 26 25 24 23 22 21

For Kim,

For embodying the Radiant Light of Jesus

CONTENTS

INTRODUCTION

A Dim Light

"SOMETHING ISN'T RIGHT."

There's been a time or two in my life when I've visited my physician and said those very words. Usually, some odd symptoms will show up that cause me to feel a little bit off. Several years ago I had convinced myself I was experiencing heart failure. That may sound overdramatic, except my symptoms seemed to be quite serious.

I was always exhausted no matter what I did. My husband would be content with seven hours of sleep, but I seemed to need ten. My hair started to fall out, and my skin was pale. I was once a triathlete and could run for miles, but even walking up a flight of stairs caused me to be winded.

I then noticed that my heart rate would skyrocket when doing the slightest things like standing up and walking to the next room. Even preaching became difficult.

"Something just isn't right," I told the doctor. I explained my symptoms, we ran some tests, and it turned out I was severely anemic.

When I look at the dearly beloved bride of Christ in North America, I see enough concerning symptoms for me to say, "Something just isn't right." I'm concerned about us.

CHICAGOLAND

I grew up in the peak of the 1990s youth ministry culture—think DC Talk, Jennifer Knapp, Switchfoot, WWJD bracelets, street evangelism, and my very own homemade bubble paint T-shirt that said "Jesus Freak."

At sixteen I had a genuine thirst and love for Jesus, my newly discovered Lord and Savior. I grew up in a home of good, cultural Christians. I was baptized and confirmed in a mainline church. Sometime around my freshman year of high school, I developed a thirst for a more meaningful understanding of God. I'm not sure what the trigger was, other than the prevenient grace of God. There was also a sense of curiosity about some of the things I heard from the Christians in school. Something about them was remarkably different. They were close to one another, and I longed for the sense of belonging and community they exuded. They talked about Jesus in almost mystical ways, and I wanted the same experience.

So there I was, in the late nineties, standing in the back of a log cabin—the meeting house for Campus Life—searching for an answer for my yearning. Youth leaders and students testified about the goodness of Jesus, and I wanted more. Soon after, one of the youth leaders invited me to begin reading my Bible, so I did—cover to cover. Every night, as fast as I could, I would race up to my bedroom to plow my way through the story of God. I was completely captivated.

When I arrived at the Gospel of Luke, my mind could hardly comprehend the goodness of Jesus and the horror of the cross. But there in my bedroom, I said yes to Jesus. I had no idea of how that moment would set the trajectory of my life, but it did—drastically.

As a newly minted Jesus freak, I was ready to set the world on fire for Jesus. I started with my own high school. Every week I would illegally pack eleven kids in my Toyota RAV4 and bring them to Campus Life. Mondays were my favorite day of the week. I would come to a school on Mondays with a stack of fliers for Campus Life, and I would leave school empty-handed with a car full of kids. I wanted the world to know Jesus as I knew him. Church was my haven of rest and peace; it was the place I wanted to be nearly every waking moment. If you would have told me the church had flaws, I would have fiercely defended it.

When I first learned about Billy Graham, I wanted to be just like him, but only because Billy was telling people about Jesus by the multitudes. Then I heard about Bill Hybels. Somewhere around 2001, I joined a carload of students to drive an hour north to the Willow Creek campus in Barrington, Illinois. When I walked into the lobby, I saw escalators and food courts. When I walked into the massive ten thousand-plus seat sanctuary, the hair on my arms stood up. Someone gets to preach to this many people every week?

From that day on, Willow Creek Community Church was the epitome of success—through the eyes of a new Christian formed in Western evangelicalism—in the economy of the kingdom: church growth, large buildings, and bodies in seats. In my mind this was the golden vision every pastor ought to strive for.

When I began my journey in ministry in the early 2000s as a Youth for Christ director, we used to compare attendance numbers in staff meetings and then high-five one another when attendance was "crushing it."[1] There's hardly a pastor that would deny feelings of excitement when numbers are unusually high or when the pastor glances out in the sanctuary and the seats are full. Needing to build more prominent and more state-of-the-art sanctuaries can be a thrill, no doubt.

In my early days of ministry, I recall attending a church growth summit, and as a young associate pastor, I was enamored by one pastor's account of growing a church from sixty to five hundred people. I couldn't take notes fast enough and couldn't wait to someday apply the tactics I learned that day. With a quick scroll through Google, we can learn all about the "easy principles to church growth."

Numbers tend to be quite a big deal for pastors. This can be a helpful metric and is something we celebrate for a good reason. As someone who has been so profoundly impacted by the gospel of Jesus, I celebrate anytime someone decides to follow Jesus for the first time. I celebrate when lives are transformed within the body of Christ. I celebrate every time someone is newly baptized. These are just some of the few reasons I do what I do. Simultaneously, an emphasis on numbers as the golden metric for success can become unhealthy, especially when we pursue success at the expense of faithfulness or appearance at the expense of authentic community.

After serving in ministry for quite some time and after attending seminary, I developed a more robust kingdom theology, ecclesiology, and pneumatology. I knew deep down that the metrics of empire weren't necessarily the fruit of goodness in the kingdom. I knew it, but it was still so deeply ingrained in the mind of this young pastor.

PASADENA, CALIFORNIA

In 2016 I accepted the new role as senior pastor of First Church of the Nazarene of Pasadena, affectionately known as "PazNaz."

PazNaz is a large and historic church in Southern California with a rich history in Pasadena as well as the Nazarene denomination. However, upon my arrival many left the church, and although there were compounding factors, some of it was over the sheer fact that I am a woman. Many just "couldn't do a woman pastor" even if their theology agreed with it. For others it was a straight-up "abomination" and "sin." Some believed that "PazNaz is doomed for failure and will lose the favor of God because they called a woman." Many simply could not comprehend a young thirty-something woman taking on such a significant role "with small children at home."

Many stayed, rallied, prayed, and jumped all in for the mission. Those that stayed are some of the godliest, most loving, and most faithful people you'll ever meet. But they too were trying to comprehend the scale of loss. Many were concerned about the sheer loss. The bottom dropped out of the place, some shared. Concerned members lamented, "Pastor, how will we fill the sanctuary again?" which I interpreted as, "When will we be successful again?"

It has taken much prayer and therapy for me to recognize that the loss didn't mean the church was wrecked, and for that matter, it wasn't Tara Beth Leach who wrecked this precious church. What I was experiencing was symptomatic of something much bigger.

THE PROBLEM WITH OUR METRICS

I began to discover that hidden behind the curtains of evangelicalism's golden crowns of success was a malnourished vision for flourishing in the kingdom. Not only was it malnourished but when lived out, there were problems and disappointments, and sometimes it produced fruit that was the antithesis to the vision laid out in Scripture. Perhaps "success" wasn't what we thought it was.

Furthermore, what we have discovered in many of evangelicalism's successful megachurches is that behind closed doors of rising attendance, building, and cash, the situation isn't what it seems. Take, for example, Willow Creek, Harvest Bible Chapel, and the Southern Baptist Convention. The curtains were pulled back and the light shined in the darkness. We all saw moral failures happening behind closed doors in some of America's largest churches.

It turns out we had been using the wrong metric all along. Suddenly, we all had to come to terms with the reality that what was once anointed as a success wasn't successful after all. These old metrics only told some of the story.

Imagine going into a doctor with chest pains and the doctor pulling out a stethoscope. After listening for a moment, the doctor says, "Your heart is beating rhythmically. I think you're in great shape!" I imagine that you would explain to the doctor that more sophisticated measuring tools are needed. The stethoscope shows only part of the picture.

Or imagine going to the doctor for your child's yearly checkup, and the doctor measures *only* the child's weight and height. If the doctor were to declare your child healthy but your child has aches and pains on a regular basis, you'd ask for more tests.

We are acting like this doctor by measuring the health of the church numerically. Of course, measuring numerically is far easier than measuring faithfulness or love or kindness or hospitality or integrity. Measuring numerically is low-hanging fruit. At the same time, what if our measuring system has been covering up symptoms for *decades*, and only recently are we coming to terms with the severity of the crisis?

You see, it isn't just about Willow Creek, Harvest Bible Chapel, and the Southern Baptist Convention. It isn't only about evangelicals' propensity for partisan politics. We could find many symptoms: #ChurchToo, segregation, polarization, hypernationalism within local church worship, and a history of systemic racism. These didn't happen overnight; rather, they are symptomatic of a crisis that has been brewing for decades.

The erosion of the witness in the church began to crumble years ago, and today we are trying to make sense of it all. Through all of this there have been ongoing conversations on the post-Christian context. There is a notable shift happening in churches and communities all around America. PazNaz has been around for decades, which means many of its members have been around for long enough to talk about what they call "the good old days." To them, the "good old days" are the days when "most people went to church." Now, most people don't go to church.

Many look for somewhere or someone to point the finger at, and the finger is often pointed outward instead of inward. Blame the millennials, blame the erosion of Christian morals in America, blame the liberals, blame immoral presidents, blame the decay of culture.

Perhaps we are pointing in the wrong direction. Maybe we ought to honestly and humbly look in the mirror and turn the finger back toward ourselves. Maybe it isn't the post-Christian culture, and instead we have a post-Christian *church*. Maybe it's time for *us* to look in the mirror, examine our hearts, and ask the Lord to show us where we've fallen short, confess, lament, and repent.

LET'S GET UNCOMFORTABLE

I can remember back when I was a young student studying to be in ministry; whenever someone would critique the church, I got uncomfortable. *Don't talk about my family like that*, I'd think. *Don't talk about the very people that birthed me, nurtured me, fed me, and formed me.* But these days I can see the ways that systems of evil have entrapped us, and I yearn for the church to break free from the systems that entangle us and experience the free, full, flourishing life that Jesus came to teach, live, die, and ascend to the throne for. We were meant for so much more than this. But before we experience freedom, we need to first be uncomfortable. It's time to name some things, lament some things, repent of some things, and step into new wineskins.

No longer can we ignore our symptoms or turn a blind eye. It's time we courageously poke at the things that may sting a little. Actually, you may get angry, and I'll be honest, that makes me a bit nervous. I once heard someone say that good rabbis make their listeners mad. If a doctor pokes and prods and I suddenly yell, "Ouch!" then the doc has exposed a painful symptom. I'm not a rabbi, and I'm certainly not a doctor, but I do see concerning symptoms these days. I'd rather poke than turn a blind eye.

But after some of the poking, I want you to know how much I think Jesus believes in us. I actually think it's a gift that our symptoms are being exposed. Perhaps the curtains are being pulled back so that the Spirit might do a new thing in our midst. Perhaps this wilderness will bring us to our knees so we might experience new humility, new dependence, and new freedom. Lisa Sharon Harper says it best about evangelicals:

> What if the process of repentance—restitution and repair—is the way of God, the narrow road to the health of our world?
>
> And what if repentance is the way to the restoration of the image of God in a people twisted by hubris?[2]

WHO AM I CRITIQUING?

I am a child of White evangelicalism, and I am speaking primarily to both pastors and lay leaders of the White evangelical church. While I know that not all evangelicals are White and certainly have diversity, I am speaking to a generation of believers who have historically worshiped in White evangelical churches. It is my hope that we as pastors and leaders can name and acknowledge the places where we have become entrapped by "the powers not of this world." The apostle Paul names this for us, "Our struggle is not against flesh and blood, but against the rulers, against the authorities, against the powers of this dark world and against the spiritual forces of evil in the heavenly realms" (Eph 6:12).

There is indeed a struggle happening within the White evangelical church; there are places where we are under the grips of dark powers of this world. It's time we move away from dismissiveness and denial, and face reality. I hope that we don't just name our problems, but I pray this brings us to our knees. I pray we lament, confess, and repent. I pray we lean into the creative and missional imagination of the triune God. Lisa Sharon Harper poses an important and uncomfortable question for us, "What if the call to White evangelicals is to stop trying to be God, to control everything and everyone and to join the rest of humanity—the beloved dust? . . . Will lament lead to surrender?[3]

Are you squirming yet? I am.

Dear reader, perhaps you find yourself a bit uncomfortable like I was years ago. I get that. The church is my family. Week in and week out I get to worship with, journey with, and live in a mutually edifying relationship with a local church. The church is the radiant bride of Christ, and I too get defensive when others trample on the bride's garment. But the way I see it, the bride's garment is tangled up and entrapped in ways that are holding us back from the free, full, and flourishing life we were meant to live.

I pray you hear my words like a mother or aunt who deeply loves her family and wants to see her family live into its full potential—that is, the radiant church in all its beauty. I believe the *whole church* is called to total radiance, and while I may be critiquing what is primarily White evangelicalism, I am calling the whole church to radiance. May we come alongside our brothers and sisters of color and partner to be radiant people.

WHO IS RADIANT?

The writer of Hebrews says this about Jesus, "The Son is the radiance of God's glory and the exact representation of his being, sustaining all things by his powerful word. After he had provided purification for sins, he sat down at the right hand of the Majesty in heaven" (Heb 1:3). Jesus is in the radiant image of the glory of our majestic God. No one is fully radiant but God, and we see this embodied in the person of the radiant King Jesus. We are the bride of the King, called to bear witness to this radiant gospel and this radiant kingdom where Jesus rules. In Christ, we are brilliantly radiant. Throughout history, Jesus' radiant bride has shined with luster and brilliance, but at times it has waned. As a pastor I lament when our light is pale, and I rejoice when we shine with brilliance. There is nothing more that I long for than a radiant church that blazes in the darkness. My hope is that throughout these pages I'll be able to name the places our light is diminished, and paint a vision for a church that illuminates in a weary world.

I write this book with much fear and trembling, but also with a push from the Spirit that I can't ignore. So I can't think of a better way to start this book than with a prayer.

Lord, I am ill-equipped to write this book, and yet words are birthing in my mind and heart that I can't seem to shake. So I give the pages of this book to you. I pray this book will be a tool to help expand the imagination of the church. Help us to see, name, and flee from the things that entrap us, and help us to lean into the radiant vision of the kingdom rooted in Scripture, held together by the covenant of God the Father, fulfilled by King Jesus, and birthed by the Spirit. Amen.

QUESTIONS FOR INDIVIDUALS AND GROUPS

1. What do you love about the church?

2. Considering there is not a perfect church, and the church is certainly imperfect, what are some of the symptoms you notice of the imperfect church?

3. In what ways has the church ignored the symptoms? How has this been harmful?

4. In what ways has the church measured success that has been harmful?

5. In what ways has the church measured success that has been helpful?

6. What are your laments for the church?

7. What are your hopes for the church?

1

THE CALL TO RADIANCE

"You're not one of those born-again Christians, are you?"

I wasn't sure how to answer that question. Was it a trap? What did they think "born-again" meant? I leaned over the fence that stood between my neighbor and me, and we both watched our children play together in the yard. "What do you mean by that?" I tried to ask in the most nonjudgmental tone as possible and instead take the posture of curiosity. "Well, those born-agains talk about a God who loves you, but they live their lives as anything but loving. They only care about their own political agenda and not the people that they have politicized." I can't remember exactly how I navigated the conversation that day, but perhaps it's familiar to you.

Some circles project hostility between the church and culture. While plenty of people have the opposite and more loving view of the church, I think it's safe to say that there's a growing tension between the church and culture in the Western world.

There's been a pulling away of sorts, however. No longer do we enjoy easy approval from Western culture, and going to church on Sunday mornings is no longer the thing to do. According to Gallup, the most dramatic shift is those who don't identify as religious at all.[1]

Aside from decline, our reputation has been put to the test. If we were to dial the conversation back to 2007, David Kinnaman, president of the Barna Group, noted this from an outsider to Christianity, "Most people I meet assume that Christian means very conservative, entrenched in their thinking, anti-gay, anti-choice, angry, violent, illogical, empire builders, they want to convert everyone, and they generally cannot live peacefully with anyone who does not believe what they believe."[2] A few years later, in 2011, David Fitch declared that evangelicalism was coming to an end. He writes, "Evangelicalism's influence within American society is painfully on the wane. As recent as just this past decade, evangelicalism had carried a significant amount of political influence within society and seemed confident of its identity as a church in America."[3]

The influence the church once had is waning, the light that once shined bright is diminishing, and the salt that was once salty is losing its saltiness.

Over a decade ago, as many influential church leaders and theologians saw the future of the church they gathered to create manifestos. Many called for a redefining, a rebirthing, and a re-identification of the church. It was time for renewal and revival, and for the evangelical church to embrace the God who births new things. Fast forward a decade and it would appear that the church has missed the moment, or perhaps it's something that "gets worse before it gets better." Either way, I think it's safe to say we have reached a crisis moment.

The crisis, however, is not just the decline of those who declare faith in King Jesus—though that is certainly to be lamented. The crisis, instead, is an issue that must be dealt with in our own family room. This is not the time to point the finger outward, and it's not the time to blame the world. Instead, I pray that we take this opportunity to look in the mirror.

SYMPTOMS OF THE CRISIS

Moral failures. In the last few years, moral failures of pastors and so-called Christian politicians alike are being brought to light at a rapid rate. But what's troubling is how quickly we defend the perpetrator rather than the victim. Perhaps even more troubling is that at times the *world* is defending the victim while the *church* defends the perpetrator. This was an alarming reality when Bill Hybels was first accused of sexual abuse and harassment from a number of female staffers at Willow Creek. The leadership was sadly quick to defend their pastor and blame the victims. Rachel Held Evans tweeted this about the #ChurchToo movement, "The Church in America, and specifically evangelicals, are going to have to muster up some humility and take a serious look at how patriarchy, sexism, and toxic masculinity have infected their culture."[4]

In many ways it would appear that the curtains have been pulled back on systems of power—power often held by my brothers in Christ—that are wrapped in toxic systems. We have learned in recent years that behind closed doors things weren't what they appeared to be behind the glimmer and glamor of the large auditoriums, fog machines, and rapid growth of butts in the auditorium seats. Maybe all along the very things we anointed as success weren't successful after all.

Then we started to hear whispers from the mouths of trembling, broken, and fearful women. At first we asked them to keep quiet; we must not ruin the witness of the church. Some quieted down, and some got louder. When American culture started the #MeToo movement, the church had its own movement, #ChurchToo. Thousands of stories emerged—gut-wrenching, painful, and devastating stories. Take a moment to scroll through Twitter's #ChurchToo feed and grab a box of tissues while you read. If it doesn't make you weep, I don't know what will.

Many did gather 'round to listen while others continued to silence the voices of the hurting. Some who held the power had plenty of opportunities to call for the church to repent, apologize, and work toward reconciliation. I was especially grateful for leaders like Dan Meyer, senior pastor of Christ Church of Oak Brook, JR Rozko, director of Missio Alliance, Rich Villodas, pastor of New Life Fellowship in Queens, New York, and New Testament scholar Scot McKnight for the ways they and countless others prophetically called the church to confession, lament, and a better way.

Allegiance. And then the curtains were pulled back on our own allegiance. I think somewhere along the way we got confused. Of course, the history of this is deeply rooted. Is it God and country? Is my citizenship first in the kingdom of God or in my country? Or are they the same? Flags on altars next to the cross were on equal footing, and the gospel according to the empire began to collide with the gospel of King Jesus. The church fell in love with the empire, and the witness suffered because it wasn't sure which was which. Patriotism trumped the values of the kingdom, and eventually it seems we developed multiple personality disorder. On the one hand, we loved Jesus and the gift of salvation, and on the other, we sought more power, more strength, more dominance, more prestige, more wealth, more flourishing, and more gain. Eugene Cho warned,

> I would submit that the greatest challenge is actually within Christianity: It's the temptation to build the structures and institutionalism of Christianity but without the parallel commitment to Jesus. It's politicians and even Christian pastors and leaders who sprinkle on a pinch of Jesus into our thinking, speeches, or sermons but often in a way that fulfills our agenda or goals. In other words, using Jesus to promote nationalism is simply not the way of Jesus.[5]

We abandoned the imagination of Scripture and instead adopted a Western political imagination that we tried to keep firmly hitched to the Christian way. But if we were honest, it's a dimly lit version of the early church—if lit at all.

A polarized church. Instead of falling to our knees, we took to larger platforms and louder megaphones to make our views known. We took to Twitter with hateful words and memes. Instead of peacemaking, we took to dividing and violent speech. We were more interested in being right than unified, so we drew harder lines in the sand and pushed the weak, marginalized, and hurting away.

Meanwhile, young ears were listening, and young eyes were watching. What was meant to be beautiful slowly eroded away. As the pastor of the second oldest church in my denomination, many grandparents are lamenting over the decline of the attendance of young people, and many are fearful for the future of the church. Perhaps many decided that the radiance of the church wasn't what they thought it was.

IT'S NOT THEM; IT'S US

No longer can we point the finger away from ourselves and put the blame on culture wars. No longer can we say, "It's because they took God out of our schools," and, "That generation is ruining everything!" Instead, dear Christians, we have a few things to sort through and talk about.

We've been exposed, and the curtains have been pulled back. Instead of saying, "To hell with the church!" I cling to the promise of Scripture that declares, "The gates of hell shall not prevail against [the church!]" (Mt 16:18 KJV). I know how this story ends, and I know that the bride of Christ will never fully crumble. I hope that this exposure would lead us to our knees, crying out for the Spirit to birth something new, alive, beautiful, and radiant.

I believe this more than anything: what isn't revealed can't be healed. It's time to embrace what has been revealed and lean into a new kind of healing that can only be explained by the faithful presence of Jesus.

BORN-AGAIN

Somewhere in the mid-1990s, when I was a new Christian, I came across a popular bronze statue by Dean Kermit Allison. The sculpture was called "Born Again," and it depicted a man shedding his old self with a bronze layer of skin, and his new self was being born anew as a radiant, glassy, crystal version. I remember staring at that statue mesmerized and in tears. I was the statue, I thought. Newly in love with Jesus and recently beginning my life in Christ, God was doing a radiant new thing in my life. But today, that statue seems more prophetic, and it tugs at my heartstrings as I long for the church of the future.

I pray that the church would begin to see, acknowledge, and name the bronze layers that are saturated with worldly beliefs and behaviors and flee from them. I pray that the church would know that we have not been destroyed—it's not too late. I pray that we would reclaim, be renewed and revived, and allow the work of the Spirit to birth something new and radiant. Like the bronze statue, may the layers of our own systems that have hurt and harmed others begin to peel away, and may the lamp of truth, love, and righteousness be placed firmly on its pedestal and shine in all of its illuminating beauty. Not beauty for the glory of ourselves but for the glory and majesty of our King and Creator. May we shine in such a way that instead of hard lines in the sand being drawn, those who once felt excluded are now drawn to the radiant light of the church.

But birthing isn't easy work. It's painful, it's laborious, it's long, and it literally brings blood, sweat, and tears. On the early morning of April 17, 2010, I woke up at 6 a.m. to discover that my water had broken. Fortunately, I wasn't feeling any pain yet, so I decided I could take a shower, put on makeup, and grab breakfast on the way to the hospital. By the time my husband and I arrived at Panera to pick up some breakfast on the way, the labor pains began to kick in. I'll also confess that I had no idea that when the water breaks, it isn't just a one-time occurrence; rather, it keeps on coming. This was rather problematic standing in line for my bagel. After a minute or two of waiting in line, I turned to Jeff with my lips curled and my teeth together and said, "We have to go *now!*"

By the time we got to the hospital, I was in full-blown labor. Before having Caleb, I thought of myself as a tough woman with high pain tolerance. Turns out, labor was much more painful and difficult than any friend or textbook or Lamaze class could have prepared me for.

At one point during labor, my husband and parents were in the hospital room having a good old time, sharing, eating, laughing, and watching *Ghostbusters* on TV. I was angry that I was suffering and they were enjoying the moment. My husband came over to me with an angelic and peaceful look on his face, gently put his hand on my shoulder, and said, "Hey, babe, I was thinking that the next baby . . ." and before he could even finish his sentence, I angrily interrupted him with what probably seemed like demon eyes and the voice of his worst nightmares, "*Next baby? Next baby? You think I'm going to go through this again? There will be no next baby!*"

Perhaps the scariest and most challenging moment came during what many call transitional labor, which is the stage between active labor—labor pains that are a few minutes apart—and actually having to push for delivery. It's intense, and the only way for any sort of relief is to *push and potentially scream*. I did both. The nurses and my family surrounded me saying things like, "Breathe, and keep your eye on the prize! Caleb is coming! Breathe; keep your eye on the prize! Focus! Caleb is coming!"

Breathe. Keep your eye on the prize. Breathe. Breathe. Breathe. Dear church, creation is groaning. The labor pains can no longer be ignored. It's time to push and birth something new, something radiant, something wrapped in love, truth, and grace.

There is nothing glorious about labor; there is nothing easy about pushing. It hurts. It's hard. But push we must. That is, we must repent, we must name, we must rid ourselves of toxic systems, and we must abandon the imagination of the principalities and powers of this world. Let us push, breathe, keep our eyes on Jesus, press in, lean in, and reclaim the radiant vision that comes alive in Scripture.

A CALL TO RADIANCE

In Matthew 5, Jesus steps on a mount and begins to teach. His prophetic words are drenched in love and wrapped in vision. It was a sermon unlike any other that has now found its home in what we call the Sermon on the Mount (Mt 5–7). In it, Jesus shares his dreams for the already-but-not-yet people of God in Christ. He paints a vivid vision of how the people of God are to live, love, act, and care for one another. His words are no doubt piercing, and they likely make us squirm at times, but what Jesus proclaims is an illuminating and radiant vision for the bride of Christ.

Jesus' words are no mere suggestion; rather, they are passionate and piercing commands for the people of God to live into no matter where they live.[6] That is, those who are citizens of the kingdom of God.

Following Jesus' declaration of those who make the list of the blessed life, Jesus calls the church to lean into the radiant vision of the church. He calls us salt and light.

> You are the salt of the earth. But if the salt loses its saltiness, how can it be made salty again? It is no longer good for anything, except to be thrown out and trampled underfoot.
>
> You are the light of the world. A town built on a hill cannot be hidden. Neither do people light a lamp and put it under a bowl. Instead, they put it on its stand, and it gives light to everyone in the house. In the same way, let your light shine before others, that they may see your good deeds and glorify your Father in heaven. (Mt 5:13-16)

Like other popular passages of Scripture, we sometimes miss out on the fullness of what Jesus is calling us to. Often we read this passage through the lens of *I* instead of *we* and then interpret it as, "I should do more good deeds." However, this prophetic declaration of Jesus should push and pull the church into the radiant church it was meant to be. While one star is certainly something to behold, a sky full of sparkling stars is stunning. Our witness is corporate, found within congregations and communities. Our witness is a collective presence and voice and light rather than individuals.

This passage isn't a random call to do good things; rather, we are called to lean into the missional imagination of the triune God—that is, the imagination that unfolds beginning in the book of Genesis.

WE ARE THE STARS

In the first eleven chapters of Genesis, the problem of sin, brokenness, darkness, and evil is rather glaring. Murder, betrayal, division, pride, and havoc, even from Mother Nature, are just a few examples. However, we don't observe a planless God scrambling to heal God's broken creation, and neither do we observe God lashing out in anger. Instead, we discover a redemptive God who moves in with acts of love and grace. By the time we arrive at Genesis 11, we discover the beginnings of God's rescue operation. God doesn't run from the problem of sin; rather, God moves in and addresses it.

God calls Abram and Sarai to a foreign land, a place of discomfort, in a posture of trust. Without the full picture, Abram shows us a life of faithfulness, even in the midst of ruggedness and the unknown. God then unveils this grand plan:

The LORD had said to Abram, "Go from your country, your people and your father's household to the land I will show you.

> "I will make you into a great nation,
>   and I will bless you;
> I will make your name great,
>   and you will be a blessing.
> I will bless those who bless you,
>   and whoever curses you I will curse;
> and all peoples on earth
>   will be blessed through you." (Gen 12:1-3)

Through a series of trials, tests, and tribulations, Abram and Sarai learn the radical call to faithfulness. Though they constantly sought reassurance from God and showed many symptoms of doubt and distrust, they continued to put one foot in front of the other. God appeared to Abram with a fuller and more radiant vision of the role Abram's family would soon play: "Sovereign LORD, what can you give me since I remain childless and the one who will inherit my estate is Eliezer of Damascus?" Abram said, "You have given me no children; so a servant in my household will be my heir" (Gen 15:2-3).

But then the Lord responds and assures the doubting Abram: "This man will not be your heir, but a son who is your own flesh and blood will be your heir." The Lord took Abram outside and said, "Look up at the sky and count the stars—if indeed you can count them." Then the Lord said to Abram, "So shall your offspring be. Abram believed the LORD, and he credited it to him as righteousness" (Gen 15:5-6).

Abram and God then partake in an incredibly bizarre but telling covenant ceremony that included blood and animal halves.

What we discover, however, is just how deathly serious God is about keeping God's end of the covenant. That is, that God would be faithful to bless Abram's family and bless the world through God's family.

As a result of this covenant, God's people would shine brightly as they live counterculturally in a decaying world. By living out the covenant demands, the world would see the goodness of this covenant community, and the character of God would be revealed in attractive ways.

As the story goes, however, time and again the people of God harden their hearts and fail to keep up their end of the covenant. And yet God moves in, God calls, God summons the people of God to return. But they struggle to do just that.

JESUS IS THE BRIGHTEST STAR

Then, somewhere on the margins of Bethlehem, a child is born. A bright star attracted magi from the East who wanted to see the astonishing light for themselves. Right in the middle of chaos, decay, darkness, and oppression, this child moves into the neighborhood filled with chaos and he shines. The new Israel, the second Adam, fully divine and fully human, prophet and priest, and the fulfillment of all of Israel's history, reveals the very heartbeat and character of God. And we discover just how serious God is about keeping this covenant.

This King, after living a perfect life of love, healing, revelation, and wonders, meets his death on a cross. And there on the cross, the end of an evil era collides with the nails, the crown of thorns, and the body broken. And every spring the church gathers together to proclaim the good news, "He's not dead! He's alive!" We join the chorus of angels and the sermon of Mary at the tomb, "He's alive!" The King is raised to new life, and the floodgates burst forth. We discover the promises to Abram are now fulfilled, and we are the stars in the sky. No longer is ethnic Israel the only recipient of God's blessing; the dividing wall has been destroyed, and Jews and Gentiles, men and women, and slaves and free persons are all one in Christ. The re-creation of a people of God is expanded to all who are in Christ. The apostle Paul says, "Therefore, if anyone is in Christ, the new creation has come: The old has gone, the new is here!" (2 Cor 5:17). And the apostle Peter says, "You are a chosen people, a royal priesthood, a holy nation, God's special possession, that you may declare the praises of him who called you out of darkness into his wonderful light. Once you were not a people, but now you are the people of God; once you had not received mercy, but now you have received mercy" (1 Pet 2:9-10).

WE ARE CALLED TO SHINE

Paul says to the Philippians, "Do everything without grumbling or arguing, so that you may become blameless and pure, 'children of God without fault in a warped and crooked generation.' Then you will shine among them like stars in the sky" (Phil 2:15). We are the stars in the sky—shining in all of our radiant glory as the love of God bursts forth. We—all who are in Christ—are the royal priesthood and God's special possession. And the news only gets better! In Christ, we begin to reflect God's glorious image as Paul says, "And we all, who with unveiled faces contemplate the Lord's glory, are being transformed into his image with ever-increasing glory, which comes from the Lord, who is the Spirit" (2 Cor 3:18).

We are heirs of God's promises to Abraham, and we are included in God's blessed people. And just as God called Abraham to faithfulness and obedience, God also called the church. As children of Abraham and sons and daughters of the King, we've distorted the story of the perfect gospel to be a ticket to heaven—or else. But the radiant gospel is about a people leaning into and reflecting the goodness of God to an embattled world. The radiant gospel is about the people of God in Christ extending the table and gathering as an alternative community in a world gone awry. We are to embody the power of blessing—that in the middle of a chaotic, prideful, sinful, decaying, embattled, broken world, we would embody the promises of Abraham and live the vision of Jesus as salt and light. As a covenant community in Christ, we don't just randomly do salt-and-light kind of things; rather, we *are* salt and light. As salt and light, we are called to mediate the goodness, light, love, and holiness of God. What a radiant call God has entrusted to God's people.

A DIMLY LIT STAR

However, Jesus declares this word with a warning: "But if the salt loses its saltiness, how can it be made salty again? It is no longer good for anything, except to be thrown out and trampled underfoot" (Mt 5:13). A very honest, practical, and difficult warning for the church. Jesus reminds the church that there is a strong possibility of a diminished witness and impact. We see this repeatedly with moral failures in Christian leaders and pastors. When their sins are exposed, their witness abruptly crumbles and rarely returns. Let's expand this thought for the church in North America. If we damage the impact we have been entrusted with, will it ever be regained?

Dear church, we have been invited to participate in such a marvelous mission, which was first unfolded with Abraham, was revealed in the pages of Scripture, and culminated in King Jesus. This mission is still unfolding in our weary world, and the marvelous wonder of it all is that we are summoned to participate. Have we been too busy worrying about being correct instead of loving? Have we been consumed with being in control and in power rather than laying down our lives? It seems we have been more wrapped up in the ABCs of empire (attendance, building, cash) than we have in participating in the mission of God. Do we love the thrill of power at the expense of loving our neighbor? It seems we have bought into a warped vision for the Christian life. Money and consumerism are central to our vision for the good life. We sometimes bow at the altar of nationalism. Have we forgotten who we are?

When I was in high school, I was a competitive swimmer— very competitive. At the end of the day, I was interested in winning. During my senior year of high school, it was possible I would be conference champ in two different events. However, we knew that the results would be close.

Like most typical angsty teenagers, I was a train wreck at home. I projected my anxious emotions onto my family and made everyone in the house miserable. Eventually, my dad sat me down and gave me a talk:

> Tara Beth, we are so proud of you. We are amazed that you have made it to this place of perhaps being conference champ. But there's one important thing you seemed to have forgotten. You are a Moore. You might think that your role is to win. Winning is great. But as a Moore, your job isn't to win. Your job is to give it all you got—both at home and in the pool. Yes, you are fearless, you are strong, and you are determined. And you are also a Moore, which means your

character and attitude at home matters. It's not what you win or achieve; it's who you are.

That day, Dad reminded me of who I was. At the end of the day, it wasn't about the medals, but it was about my character and the name I bore. He interrupted my winning imagination and reminded me not to forget who I was.

Dear church, have we forgotten who we are? That is, have we forgotten who we are as mediators of God's goodness and love in this world? Have we forgotten the name of Jesus that we bear? The name of Jesus who bears the vision of humility and love, as Paul reminds us in Philippians 2,

> Who, being in very nature God,
>> did not consider equality with God something
>>> to be used to his own advantage;
> rather, he made himself nothing
>> by taking the very nature of a servant,
>> being made in human likeness.
> And being found in appearance as a man,
>> he humbled himself
>> by becoming obedient to death—
>> even death on a cross!
> Therefore God exalted him to the highest place
>> and gave him the name that is above every name,
> that at the name of Jesus every knee should bow,
>> in heaven and on earth and under the earth,
> and every tongue acknowledge that Jesus Christ is Lord,
>> to the glory of God the Father. (vv. 6-11)

This is the name we bear. I believe we have forgotten, and I believe it's time to return to the radiant vision of the gospel. It's time to reclaim what it means to be salt and light in this world and peel away the layers of worldly bronze and be the church that draws the attention of the world in such a way that

> at the name of Jesus every knee should bow,
>> in heaven and on earth and under the earth,
> and every tongue acknowledge that Jesus Christ is Lord,
>> to the glory of God the Father (Phil 2:10-11).

Amen.

LET US LAMENT

But before we reclaim who we are, perhaps we must confess who we've *become*. Lament is hard, uncomfortable. And the White evangelical church often avoids it. But in order to embrace our *radiant* call, we must lament the dimly lit yet powerful status quo. Lament is a powerful intrusion to the status quo. Soong-Chan Rah notes, "Lament recognizes the struggles of life and cries out for justice against existing injustices. The status quo is not to be celebrated but instead must be challenged."[7] We must confess what we've become, and we must lament. Coauthors Grace Ji-Sun Kim and Graham Hill remind us that for there to be healing, there must be lament: "Lament is about regretting and mourning the past and then moving toward repentance, justice, and a new life together."[8] Come, let us lament.

> How long, O Lord?
>
> How long will we wield power in your house for our own gain?
>
> How long will we fight for the seat of control and notoriety?
>
> How long will we embrace a vision of the good life that is a dimly lit version of the Christian life?

How long will we hoard money for prosperity at the expense
of forsaking our neighbor?

How long will we cling to toxic masculinity and femininity?

How long will we defend the perpetrator and silence the victim?

How long will we worship idols in your house of worship?

How long will we declare allegiance to gods of this world
under the banner of "in God we trust"?

How long will we sell out to the powers of this world?

You have called us to shine brighter than this.

And yet you are loving, merciful, and kind. You continue to
work, heal, and redeem in spite of us. When we abandon
obedience to you, you're still there to pursue us and pick us up.
You promise to never leave nor forsake us. Your grace is
abundant and your love unending.

Lord, we have gotten tangled up and don't know how to
untangle ourselves. We know things aren't right, but we don't
know what to do at times, so we go back to what we know and
return to the status quo. We can't seem to escape polarization,
racism, sexism, and idolatry.

Lord, we are sorry and are sad at who we have become. We
have not loved you with our whole hearts, and we have not
loved our neighbors. We have ignored our brothers and sisters
in the ditch in an effort to protect the power that we hold. We
have kept ourselves at the center when you call us to decenter
ourselves. Lord, we are troubled and long to change. We have
sinned against you. We have sinned against our neighbor.

Lord, we yearn for grace and mercy. Hear our cry of
repentance, hear our prayers and our aches of confession. We
ask that you see us and not forsake us. We pray that you would
have compassion on us and heal our brokenness.

We look to you with hope, adoration, and trust. Thank you
that you don't abandon your children but draw near to us. We

know that we have been dimly lit, and we thank you that you have continued to shine bright.

Rescue us, Lord.

Redeem us.

Heal us.

We need you.

Thank you, Lord, that on the cross you had compassion on the abusers, though it was not deserved. Thank you, Lord, that on the cross you thought of us. Thank you, Lord, that from the cross came resurrection, and you call us sons and daughters of the resurrection! Resurrect us from our slumber, and transform us into the radiant bride you believe we can be.

Amen.

QUESTIONS FOR INDIVIDUALS AND GROUPS

1. If you were to imagine a "radiant church," what does it look like?

2. When you think of "born-again Christians," what comes to mind?

3. What is the perception of "born-again Christians" in the community where you live?

4. Do you agree or disagree that the witness of the church is waning? If or if not, why?

5. What grieves you about the symptoms the author describes in this chapter?

6. When you imagine new things birthing in the church, what do you imagine?

7. What will it take for the church to shine brightly?

2

THE RADIANT STORY

Since living in California, the national park and national forest system have become a playground for our family. We love exploring the many different terrains, including forests with massive trees, beaches, and the desert. One December we had the chance to visit Sequoia National Park, which is about five hours north of Los Angeles. Sequoia National Park is a treasure in the heart of California with its massive mountain range piercing the clouds and big and ancient trees.

I remember learning about sequoia trees as a child and having difficulty grasping the size of the tree that I saw in the picture. Nothing could prepare me for seeing the giant sequoias in person.

There's something absolutely majestic about the giant sequoia. The oldest tree is 3,300 years old, and their average height is 150–289 feet with a diameter of 16–23 feet. First time I saw the sequoia named General Sherman, I was overcome with emotion and awe. How could something grow to such a size? And how could something live so long? The answer, I learned, lies within the root system and context.

When we were at a gift store in Sequoia National Park, one of my boys ran up to me with a little tin can. In it was a can that read "Giant Sequoia | Grow-A-Tree-Kit." My youngest held it up while jumping up and down, "Can we grow one? Please, I'm begging; can we grow one at home?" I took the can and assured him that we could certainly try to grow one, but we would never live to see it as big as one of the ones in the park.

We purchased it, and then curiosity got the best of me. I wondered, *Could we actually grow a giant sequoia in Los Angeles County?* So I started reading all sorts of message boards from people all over the country who gave it a try. It turns out, some folks had success, but not quite like the success of the trees in Sequoia National Park.

Sequoias, you see, must be rooted in the right environment to flourish. The tiny seedling may show some signs of growth in Los Angeles County, but in the end, the ideal climate exists in a narrow 260-mile strip of forest in the western slopes of the Sierra Nevada Mountains, somewhere between five thousand and seven thousand feet in elevation. In order to flourish to full potential, the sapling must be rooted in the right place, the right elevation, the right soil, the right context, and the right environment.

Central to the Bible's big story is a vision for the people of God to live radiant and flourishing lives. This radiant vision is not for our own gain or glory; rather, it's central to the mission of God. When the people of God flourish, the light shines bright, and the world takes notice of the beauty of the alternative community.

In Paul's letter to the church in Colossae, we see that Paul was deeply concerned that the fledgling church is rooted in the right

story. Like any context and setting, there are always competing
and even false narratives. Paul knew that for the church to emulate Jesus, it needed to be rooted in the right story.

There were stories that were forming the early church away from
the radiant vision of God's kingdom; they tugged at their very citizenship in the kingdom of God. Paul knew that if they weren't
rooted in the right story, much was at stake, and this would hinder
them from the illuminating fullness God intended.

Hear Paul's pastoral words. He writes to a community he has
never met, though his deep affection for the church in Colossae
leaps off the pages. In Colossians 2, Paul shares his longings for
the church: "My goal is that they may be encouraged in heart and
united in love, so that they may have the full riches of complete
understanding, in order that they may know the mystery of God,
namely, Christ, in whom are hidden all the treasures of wisdom
and knowledge" (Col 2:2-3).

Paul longed to see the church reach the maturity it was meant
to reach—maturity and flourishing that meant they would have
"full riches of complete understanding." Paul could see the potential and longed for the church to reach it. Like any good pastor
and prophet, Paul could see the potential dangers that could pull
them away from this radiant vision: "I tell you this so that no one
may deceive you by fine-sounding arguments. For though I am
absent from you in body, I am present with you in spirit and
delight to see how disciplined you are and how firm your faith in
Christ is" (Col 2:4-5).

Paul knew that the church in Colossae was surrounded by
competing narratives—narratives saturated with the principalities and powers of this world—that could easily uproot the
people of God from the story of God that culminates in King

Jesus. Paul knew that they were at risk of being deceived by those with a charming speech filled with deceit.

So in verse 6, Paul points them back to the right narrative: "So then, just as you received Christ Jesus as Lord, continue to live your lives in him." The word *receive* may not have the same impact for us today as it did for the early church. This word was reaching back into the oral traditions and oral law passed from one generation to the next in the people of God. In the Old Testament, Moses received the Torah and then passed it along to the elders, and the elders passed in on to the people of God and to the prophets. And this continued from one generation to the next. And now the Colossians have received the good news of Jesus Christ as Lord. This story that has been passed on to them and which they have now received is the story Paul reminds them to be rooted in. The story that this fledgling church must be rooted in has been passed down to God's people through the apostolic witness, which is rooted in King Jesus. Anything other than that story had the potential to interfere with the growth, health, and flourishing of the family tree.

Competing philosophies of the day surrounded the family tree and had the potential to seduce the believers away from the proper story—the story that declares Jesus as the one and true King and Lord. Paganism, hypernationalism, false religions, and cultural practices attempted to root the family tree in the wrong story. Paul knew that if they embraced the competing narratives, the tree would not become what it was meant to be; it would receive the wrong nutrients and would be rooted in the wrong story.

It was only when the fledgling church was rooted in the right story that its people would begin to reflect, emulate, and imitate the one they were rooted in. In other words, when rooted in the right story, the church's actions would mirror the one they claim as Lord. We can almost imagine the flourishing of a mighty giant sequoia in Paul's words. "So then, just as you received Christ Jesus as Lord, continue to live your lives in him, rooted and built up in him, strengthened in the faith as you were taught, and overflowing with thankfulness" (Col 2:6-7).

The family tree, when rooted in the right story, would be rooted, built up in strength, and overflowing with a life of thankfulness. In other words, when the church is planted in the story of Jesus, it would continuously grow stronger and stronger against the competing narratives.

We all live in a story. The story we live in is powerful and affects how we live and shapes our character and our vision for the good life. Our story orients our purpose for living. Our social environment reinforces our various stories, and they are passed down from one generation to the next. We receive them, we root ourselves in them, we grow in them, and they form us.

We must understand that it's possible to believe in Jesus and still be rooted in the wrong story.

It's possible to believe in Jesus and not have Jesus driving our lives.

It's possible to believe in Jesus and live in a way that is counter the kingdom of God.

It's possible to believe in Jesus and live nothing like Jesus.

It's possible to believe in Jesus and live as citizens of this world instead of the kingdom.

Dear church, what story are we rooted in? I have the sense that in the Western world, toxins, weeds, and false stories are leaking into our root system. If we were honest, I think we'd discover some false narratives that have tarnished our witness.

ROOTED IN INDIVIDUALISM

One of the most toxic narratives Christians in the West have been rooted in is that of individualism. While no individual is like another, and together individuals make a beautiful mosaic of color, light, and love, an overemphasis on *me* is toxic and idolatrous.

The problem isn't celebrating the beauty of individuals created in the image of God; rather, the privatization of one's personal faith nurtures an environment of consumerism and personal preference.

As a result, America in particular has cultivated soil for church splits and an environment of competition and polarization. Church history tells a troubling story as revealed in this popular joke:

Once I saw this guy on a bridge about to jump. I said, "Don't do it!"

He said, "Nobody loves me."

I said, "God loves you. Do you believe in God?"

He said, "Yes."

I said, "Are you a Christian or a Jew?"

He said, "A Christian."

I said, "Me too! Protestant or Catholic?"

He said, "Protestant."

I said, "Me too! What denomination?"

He said, "Baptist."

I said, "Me too! Northern Baptist or Southern Baptist?"

He said, "Northern Baptist."

I said, "Me too! Northern Conservative Baptist or Northern Liberal Baptist?"

He said, "Northern Conservative Baptist."

I said, "Me too! Northern Conservative Baptist Great Lakes Region or Northern Conservative Baptist Eastern Region?"

He said, "Northern Conservative Baptist Great Lakes Region."

I said, "Me too! Northern Conservative Baptist Great Lakes
Region Council of 1879 or Northern Conservative Baptist
Great Lakes Region Council of 1912?"

He said, "Northern Conservative Baptist Great Lakes
Region Council of 1912?"

I said, "Die heretic!" And I pushed him over.[1]

Christena Cleveland notes that this uncovers a dangerous and
hidden reality of the church.[2] Not only does it reveal the evils of
divisions and hostility, but it exposes one of the many symptoms
of religious individualism. When religion becomes a matter of
personal preference and choice, we lose sight of working out our
salvation with fear and trembling—in community and as a people.

Somewhere around the 1950s to 1960s, Christians began to
embrace their Christian faith as a private matter. The idea that
faith is a private matter and that Jesus is a personal or private
savior permeated the Christian mindset. Jesus was all one needed
for faith, and church became an afterthought. This poses to be a
serious crisis for the church.

Redemption has been overly personalized, and the emphasis
on a personal relationship with Jesus has created a mindset that
church is just something we do to strengthen our personal relationship with Jesus. When we divorce our Christian life from
what it means to be a people, we divorce our lives from the
Christian faith. The Christian life does not offer the option of
withdrawing from the people of God; rather, God established
covenant relationships with a *people*, not just individual persons.

Holiness has been reduced to personal piety, which is far from
the biblical vision for holiness. Instead of having a broader vision
of what it means to be a holy people, holiness has been personalized. The Christian who seeks to be holy abstains from smoking,

drinking, and sexual immorality. But in Scripture, some of the symptoms of brokenness and sin were corporate and included the lack of care for the poor and marginalized in society.

As a result, we have rooted ourselves in a distorted vision of the Christian life, which at times is a form of narcissism. The kingdom we are to root ourselves in, however, is not one of self-fulfillment or privatization but one that nurtures the self-forgetting life. It's a life of taking up our cross and denying ourselves. It is a vision of *we* more than *me*.

The bride of Christ must reimagine its posture in a rapidly changing context, returning to the biblical vision centered on the covenant people, community, and kingdom. To embrace the gospel of Jesus is to lean fully into the good news of a people as the new creation in Christ (2 Cor 5:17). As the new creation in Christ, we are invited into a new way of living and being as a newly created community. As Peter reminds us, once we were not a people, but now we are:

> You are a chosen people, a royal priesthood, a holy nation, God's special possession, that you may declare the praises of him who called you out of darkness into his wonderful light. Once you were not a people, but now you are the people of God; once you had not received mercy, but now you have received mercy. (1 Pet 2:9-10)

The Christian life is not a solo journey; instead it is a journey of covenant togetherness. This may be rather bold, but maybe an *individual Christian* is a misnomer. John C. Nugent observes, "There is no such thing as Lone Ranger Christianity."[3] Throughout the story of God, we don't see a vision for private pietism but holy people. Sure, it's messy and flawed, but that's the beauty of covenant togetherness. The church is filled with broken sinners who often struggle to get along, agree, and see eye to eye. And yet the same church is invited to *be the light* in a dark, broken, and weary world. The tasks of proclaiming the gospel, healing the sick, setting captives free, making wrongs right, feeding the hungry, clothing the naked, adopting orphans, and holding the widow have been given to the church, not loosely connected individuals.

THE STRENGTH OF OUR MISSION

The strength of our mission is not just in the power of God but also in our togetherness. Nugent says,

> Disciples stop thinking of "I can do all things through Christ who strengthens me" as just an individual confession. God strengthens us through each other. We need to think and act not only as if God is an invisible force by our side, but also as if God is visibly with us through the body of Christ. We need to move from a mentality that asks, "Can I do this with God's help?" to one that asks, "Should we do this with the resources God has given us as a body?"[4]

A *radiant* church is unified in its mission. When I was at PazNaz, we together discerned how we believed our mission could be lived out both locally and globally. Within our context, there were endless needs, but it became apparent that the two areas where we felt we could best serve our city were to care for the homeless or poor, and also the immigrant. Caring for the homeless, poor, and immigrants in our midst was a shared mission, and we had a sense that we were in this together. Different parts of the body lived this out differently, but our hearts were aligned in caring for our community. Some served by writing cards, others by packing meals every week. Some served by coming to church at 6 o'clock on a Sunday morning and making warm burritos for the homeless, and still others by fostering an unaccompanied child who may have recently crossed the border.

We didn't merely ask, "What is God asking *me* to do?" Instead we asked, "What is God asking *us* to do, and how can *we* accomplish this in God's strength?" Call me a prisoner of hope, but I believe the radiant church of the future can be who God wants us to be, but only if we do this *together*.

GATHERING IS ABOUT WE NOT ME

Sadly, at times Sunday morning worship has been hijacked by an individualistic worldview. I often hear someone say, "I'm just not getting anything out of it." Or "It wasn't feeding me." Or "I need to find a church that fills my tank." If this is how we view the Sunday morning gathering, then we might as well find the best online preacher and stay home.

What if gathering isn't only about *me*? What if gathering isn't about my own personal preference? Imagine a church that doesn't show up for me but for *us*. I don't always show up for me, but I show up for Rosa, Brooke, Sydney, Scott, Marcos, and Sarah. They show up for me too. Even as a pastor, there are some Sundays when my heart is so heavy that I need to have my brothers and sisters remind me of the story of God. I need to hear them sing praises to the God who heals weary hearts and restores the broken spaces of this world. I need others to pray when I am too weak to pray, and I need to be reminded of the God who rescued and is still rescuing.

Sunday isn't the only time to celebrate our togetherness. Our togetherness is in full bloom throughout the week. It's in full bloom when we break bread together on an ordinary Tuesday night, when we share prayer requests via texts, and when we celebrate the birth of a new child or the death of a loved one. The Christian life is not a solo journey, dear ones. As I always used to say to the beloved flock in Pasadena, "I need you. You need me. We need you. You need us."

ROOTED IN PARTISAN POLITICS

As a North American pastor, partisan politics is perhaps the most troubling, toxic, and problematic for the church in North America.[5]

These days, when I dare to log onto Facebook and scroll through my newsfeed, I more often than not see posts from well-intended Christians (let's give them the benefit of the doubt) who fill their timelines with political memes, articles, and statements. Usually, when someone posts a comment that opposes such a post, the original poster will fire back with heat, anger, and antagonism. Sometimes I get caught up reading the thread and later regret it. As I read, I take a few deep breaths and whisper to myself over and over, *Don't engage. Don't say anything. Just walk away, Tara Beth. Nothing to see here.* Most of the time I'm successful, and usually I close my computer and vow to never read a thread like that again.

After a few months of serving at PazNaz, the political landscape was boiling. It was during the 2016 elections, and while I am still young, I don't ever recall a more polarized landscape. What was most concerning to me is not just the lack of charitable discourse but a seemingly deep-seated belief that the kingdom of God is somehow enacted through Congress. So I did a preaching series on the politics of Jesus.

My mentor warned me that this would be a risky series to do so early in my pastorate, and he was probably right. But I was troubled that so many believed there could be such a thing as a Christian nation. I realized how deeply ingrained the idolatry was as I preached my sermon on the Sunday after the election.

PazNaz is diverse—generationally, culturally, socioeconomically, and politically. On the Sunday after the election, some PazNaz people were celebrating, others were weeping. We had people at peace and undocumented residents developing emergency plans for deportation. We were a divided congregation, and I was concerned. It happened to be Communion Sunday, so I stood at the Lord's Table and said:

> Over the last week, I have wondered whether we as Christians have forgotten who we are. I have observed more walls built up against one another than bridges. Anger, name-blaming, and finger-pointing.
>
> And as your pastor, I have had many conversations this week. I've had conversations with folks who felt like both choices were evil, but they are happy that at least Hillary didn't win. I've had many conversations with folks who are lamenting because to them the vote felt like a vote against women, minorities, and people of color. I've learned that there are people in our congregation that are utterly terrified for fear of being deported, terrified of families being ripped apart. I've had conversations with folks who felt obligated to vote the "Christian vote"—voting against abortion and for the conservative Supreme Court—folks who just couldn't fathom voting for abortion. I've had conversations with folks who felt neither option was a good one, so they just did the best they could. I've had conversations with

folks who still can't seem to separate God's kingdom and American politics. I've had conversations with people who are numb. I've had conversations with people who say, "If that's what evangelicals are, then I'm out." And guess what? All of these people aren't just nameless people we read on Twitter or Facebook or the news. These people are our family. Look around the room. These people are us. These people are you. Have we forgotten who we are?

The rest of my sermon I talked about love, but unfortunately, little did I know that I would watch people exit *one by one as I made my comments*. In the weeks to follow, as a new pastor to this church, I navigated some of my most challenging days to date. People left the church *on both sides*. Some said "You're too conservative! You should have spoken out against Trump." Others said, "You're too liberal and clearly voted for Hillary!" The truth is, I'm neither left nor right. To me, Jesus is Lord and King, and that settles things.

At the core of our Christian faith is the belief that God is King. Nothing more beautifully captures this than Psalm 47.

> Clap your hands, all you nations;
> shout to God with cries of joy.
> For the LORD Most High is awesome,
> the great King over all the earth.
> He subdued nations under us,
> peoples under our feet.
> He chose our inheritance for us,
> the pride of Jacob, whom he loved.
> God has ascended amid shouts of joy,
> the LORD amid the sounding of trumpets.

Sing praises to God, sing praises;
    sing praises to our King, sing praises.
For God is the King of all the earth;
    sing to him a psalm of praise.
God reigns over the nations;
    God is seated on his holy throne.
The nobles of the nations assemble
    as the people of the God of Abraham,
for the kings of the earth belong to God;
    he is greatly exalted.

While this is central to the story of God, it has also been since the first temptation to usurp God's role as King. Humanity has always wanted to not only be like God but usurp God's role as King.

In the beginning we were created to be God's representatives on earth. We were invited to rule on God's behalf. Eventually, as sin and evil entered the scene, humanity became intoxicated with the idea of *ruling*.[6] This intoxication is played out at the Tower of Babel when Israel demanded a human king, and all the times Israel disobeyed the Lord.

But then a baby is born in a not so politically silent night. The people still wanted their king, but Rome held the seat. This baby was born as the King, and while many hoped he would overthrow Rome by force and might, his journey as King was hardly even in the imagination of Israel.

Jesus assumes his role as King and proclaims himself as central to the entire story of God (Mt 5:17). Jesus begins to teach and preach about the kind of kingdom he has inaugurated, and he places himself as the King of this kingdom. He calls us to submit to *his ways* and to live in his kingdom just as he lives and teaches.

More than anything, Jesus asks for allegiance to himself and him alone. Jesus is Lord.

However, humanity continues to be intoxicated with power. We want to rule. Not only that but when we look at the broken world, we want to fix it. As a result we, like those who built the tower of Babel, seek to be *like God and fix the world.* Furthermore, we want to rule and prosper more than others. As a result, one of our greatest temptations is to usurp the role of God. This is most evident in our twisted belief that a nation-state or earthly political entity can agitate the ideals of the kingdom of God. We are wildly confused. The declaration that Jesus is Lord is a bold claim. It is bigger than saying "Jesus is Lord of my heart."

To say that Jesus is Lord means that Rome and Caesar are not. To say that Jesus is Lord as well as Caesar is idolatry. To say that Jesus is Lord and so is a political party, nation-state, or president is also idolatrous.

American Christians are confused about what is American and what is Christian, and the desire to wed the two has thwarted the church's mission and tarnished its witness. It seems that most days, American Christians are marked by today's rulers' agendas, plans, and ideas more than the Lamb's. But here is the reality: no agenda, plan, or campaign will ever heal our broken world. As the people of God in Christ, we are marked by the King. We are baptized in Christ, not red, white, and blue. No matter where we stand on the political spectrum, if we are looking for the state to enact the ideals of the kingdom, we'll be waiting for a long time—*it will never happen.*

While I am sure America's founding fathers had a faith life, to baptize a nation-state in the name of Christianity critically damages the witness of the church. When we confuse America with the bride of Christ, we damage our witness. When we entangle ourselves in the agendas of the day, we can't possibly bear witness to the crucified and risen King. We instead bear witness to war machines and the marginalization of entire people groups, and we do it with blood on our hands.

ENGAGED CITIZENS

While we are called to have allegiance to King Jesus first and foremost, that's not an invitation to ignore brokenness around us. After the 2016 election, many well-meaning Christians said something along the lines of "Don't worry about it. God is on the throne! God is in control!" However, these statements easily become an invitation to be politically disengaged and "just let things happen." To declare the lordship of Jesus is to live in God's world in God's ways no matter who is the president. To say that "Jesus is Lord" is to live under Jesus' lordship in such a way that our obedience is under the reign and rule of the lamb, not the donkey or the elephant. To believe that Jesus is Lord is to not be disengaged but engaged in the partnering with God in the redemption of all of creation. This means understanding our obligation as Christians to care for those who may be harmed, oppressed, or marginalized by political decisions.

We should be engaged and well-informed about the political landscape. Ignoring the world around us and merely waiting for the future kingdom of God ignores the Great Commandment of loving our neighbor. Eugene Cho says, "As Christians, we cannot pretend we can transcend politics and simply 'preach the gospel' if we truly want to love our neighbors and pursue faithfulness. Jesus did not call us only to be saved; He called us to follow Him—and He goes to some uncomfortable destinations."[7]

I am grateful to be an American citizen, and there's no other country I'd rather live in. Those who live in America ought to be good citizens (Rom 13). We pay our taxes, vote, and stay engaged the best we can. Our engagement ought not to be for the benefit of me alone but for the neighbors around us. Eugene Cho also says, "We live in a physical reality in which our political action or inaction impacts those around us—our neighbors. And part of the way we care for our neighbors is to respond to the circumstances affecting them."[8] Politicians regularly make decisions that potentially hurt and oppress our neighbors. Political inaction ignores the widow, orphan, immigrant, and poor at our doorstep.

NEITHER CONSERVATIVE NOR LIBERAL

I am not proposing for us to disengage from politics. Instead, I'm calling us to unwed ourselves from *partisan* politics in general. As a pastor, I am very concerned when I see extreme loyalty to red or blue. Cho says,

> The ways of the kingdom are not the ways of the world. My theology does not fit in a party platform. No single party represents me and my convictions. Therein lies the tension of trying to discern where my home is. I sometimes feel like an outsider. A fish out of water. As I see it, we must be flexible in our political leanings but inflexible with the way Jesus taught us to live and love—and that's a lot of tension. A party might claim to be the party of Christ, but no political party fully models the way of Jesus.[9]

I often confuse those on both the left and the right as I refuse to be defined by dualistic categories. To be either a conservative Christian or a liberal Christian has its problems. Unfortunately,

Christians on both sides of the aisle have little imagination for anything but one or the other. Perhaps more than ever, Christians must become nondualistic. Richard Rohr describes the dangers of dualism:

> The dualistic mind is essentially binary, either/or thinking. It knows, by comparison, opposition, and differentiation. It uses descriptive words like good/evil, pretty/ugly, smart/stupid, not realizing there may be a hundred degrees between the two ends of each spectrum. Dualistic thinking works well for the sake of simplification and conversation, but not for the sake of truth or the immense subtlety of actual personal experience. Most of us settle for quick and easy answers instead of any deep perception, which we leave to poets, philosophers, and prophets.[10]

The nondualistic Christian is able to engage politics not rooted in the ideologies of this world but through the lens of God's kingdom and God's heart. A nondualistic Christian has total loyalty and allegiance to no one but Jesus and is not bound to a single side. A nondualistic Christian is able to criticize or celebrate decisions made by any candidate or political party.

To uproot ourselves from partisan politics and root ourselves in the ways of the kingdom isn't a call to blatant disengagement; instead, it's the refusal to be wedded to a particular party and the refusal to be dualistic. Instead, when our ultimate allegiance is to King Jesus, we ought to offer a better way to those looking for an alternative—a politic not of this world but certainly in it. The people of God in Christ are to be a unique alternative in a world gone awry. Everything about us should be different from the agendas of the empire.

I long for the day Christians have conversations through the lens of Jesus' Great Commandment, not partisan politics. Worldly antagonisms, polarization, anger, and power seem to be embraced by too many. I'm not interested in a faith that chooses political party lines over love.

When COVID-19 first hit the United States, I believed for a moment that this tragic pandemic would obliterate partisan politics and unite people with a common goal of linking arms to heal our world of the virus. Instead, political news media began to create narratives on both sides, and it didn't take long for the church to be swept up in the narratives. It was clear which media Christians were listening to based on the rhetoric being repeated by pastors, leaders, and laypeople alike. Churches divided themselves against one another according to the narratives being touted by their particular political party. It was depressing that a pandemic wouldn't bring people together. Only total allegiance to Jesus and his ways will unite the people of God in Christ.

A RADIANT CHURCH LOVES AS JESUS LOVES

We need to be a church that boldly loves as Jesus loves, a church that loves fearlessly even when it is uncomfortable and scary, even when loving as Jesus loves doesn't fit a particular political party. We need to be a church that leans toward mercy and kindness. I want the messy, the uncomfortable; I want to walk in the power of the Spirit to be emboldened to love in unchartered waters. I want to be the first to say "I am wrong" if it means loving as Jesus loves. I want to be a church that chooses love. We can work this all out with fear and trembling—because we have love. We have Jesus.

ROOTED IN SUCCESS

We wouldn't be wrong to say that America bows down to the altar of success. More achievements, more stuff, more production, and more promotions are the name of the game. If we can produce good results, we get promoted. If something doesn't promise success, we'd rather avoid it. David Zahl writes, "The fixation on success occupies an expanding amount of everyday real estate."[11]

While success is a central value in American culture, the church in North America is rather enmeshed. It is deeply ingrained in who we are and what we value. The pastors most often invited to speak at conferences lead the fastest-growing and largest churches. These successful pastors often become the gurus of how to lead "successful" churches. How do we define success for churches? The larger the congregation, the bigger the budget, and the better the building means success. Those who have less are headed toward failure. Success becomes what *we* produce, and sadly, the people we are trying to reach are commodified and objectified. The people of God become a means to an end—like machines on an assembly line.

While it might feel good to have a full room and a worship space similar to a concert venue, this kind of success sadly fuels our own egos. Eugene Peterson warns against the danger of crowds in a letter to a friend who was taking on a larger church because he felt his gifts were being wasted in the smaller congregation:

> Classically, there are three ways in which humans try to find transcendence—religious meaning—apart from God as revealed through the cross of Jesus: through the ecstasy of alcohol and drugs, through the ecstasy of recreational sex, through the ecstasy of crowds. Church leaders frequently warn against the dangers of drugs and sex, but at least, in

America, almost never against crowds. . . . But a crowd destroys the spirit as thoroughly as excessive drinking and depersonalized sex. It takes us out of ourselves, but not to God, only away from him.[12]

Crowds fuel the egos of those who gathered the crowd. To be fully transparent, this is perhaps one of the most significant idols God has been chiseling away in my heart. I was once told by a member of the church that "PazNaz was once the jewel of the denomination, but now we aren't." This was couched within the reality that it's no longer a church of three thousand people. The numbers are a fraction of what they once were; therefore, we've lost something.

While we may have lost what the world calls "success," my pastor's heart can't help but notice all that we've *gained*. We've gained humility and a deeper sense of community, and this may sound strange, but we've gained discomfort. We are learning the lessons of the wilderness—that is, dependence and faithfulness even when it's uncomfortable. Attendance isn't what it was years ago, but out of that comes a spirit of surrender. In a large church, it's easy to get comfortable and slip in and out of worship on a Sunday morning, but when attendance begins to shift, the ownership of the future and mission of the church is felt by all.

This isn't always easy for me to teach a congregation when I am struggling with feelings of failure and discouragement. But as the Spirit continues to chisel away at my world-shaped heart, I am learning to truly *believe* that the world's vision for success isn't what I am supposed to lead a church into; rather, God wants our hearts, our faithfulness, our surrender, and our obedience. Better is a year of faithfulness than a year of selling out for success.

When churches bow down to the altar of success and pursue success no matter the cost, it becomes nearly impossible to not forfeit the way of the cross. This can sometimes be seen during stewardship campaigns. I've been on staff at more than one church during campaigns for building bigger and better buildings. Often, during these campaigns, the wealthiest in the church are brought in, pursued, and treated differently than the rest of the congregation. They enjoy special banquets, dinners, and extra time with the church leaders. We may have all the justifications in the world, but it's difficult to get around the teaching of James:

> My brothers and sisters, believers in our glorious Lord Jesus Christ must not show favoritism. Suppose a man comes into your meeting wearing a gold ring and fine clothes, and a poor man in filthy old clothes also comes in. If you show special attention to the man wearing fine clothes and say, "Here's a good seat for you," but say to the poor man, "You stand there" or "Sit on the floor by my feet," have you not discriminated among yourselves and become judges with evil thoughts?

> Listen, my dear brothers and sisters: Has not God chosen those who are poor in the eyes of the world to be rich in faith and to inherit the kingdom he promised those who love him? But you have dishonored the poor. Is it not the rich who are exploiting you? Are they not the ones who are dragging you into court? Are they not the ones who are blaspheming the noble name of him to whom you belong?

> If you really keep the royal law found in Scripture, "Love your neighbor as yourself," you are doing right. But if you show favoritism, you sin and are convicted by the law as lawbreakers. For whoever keeps the whole law and yet stumbles at just one point is guilty of breaking all of it. (Jas 2:1-10)

When "success" is elevated, pastors are driven to pursue the well-to-do, and the least of these become invisible, lost, ignored, and forgotten. Those who are hurting, broken, sick, and needy can easily become a distraction to the pursuit of success.

As a pastor, some of the most discouraging threats often have to do with money. The following are actual quotes I've received:

- "I don't like the change in music, so I'm pulling my tithe."
- "If you knew how much we tithed, you wouldn't be making this decision."
- "Pastor, we hear you're trying to reach young people, but they aren't the ones with the money; we are."
- "I don't like all the changes in the church, so I'm taking away my estate gift."

Money is an idol in and of itself. When it is hitched to success and one's vision of success isn't met, it is sometimes weaponized. When money is weaponized, pastors are tempted to forsake truth-telling in an effort to not upset the "constituents."

Scripture flips this idol on its head. Success in America is about gaining wealth and more followers. When success is elevated and becomes idolatrous, it is used to gain the world, no matter the cost. Jesus reminds us of the cost of discipleship, however:

> Jesus said to his disciples, "Whoever wants to be my disciple must deny themselves and take up their cross and follow me. For whoever wants to save their life will lose it, but whoever loses their life for me will find it. What good will it be for someone to gain the whole world, yet forfeit their soul? Or what can anyone give in exchange for their soul?" (Mt 16:24-26)

Success receives all the accolades, approval, and applause from the world. But the way of the cross is foolishness to the world.

The apostle Paul reminds us, "The message of the cross is foolishness to those who are perishing, but to us who are being saved it is the power of God" (1 Cor 1:18).

I can't find a single place in Scripture that says the way of the cross mirrors worldly success. We are to participate in the sufferings of Jesus. We are called to faithfulness and obedience, and sometimes that means forfeiting *success* and not the other way around.

ROOTED IN GOD'S STORY

Dear church, perhaps it's time for a great uprooting. Perhaps this shift we are feeling isn't so scary after all. What if these birth pangs are part of a great uprooting? What if God is shrinking us? What if the ground is shifting because we've rooted ourselves in the world's story sprinkled with a few of our favorite Bible verses? I'm reminded of Jesus' words at the end of his very difficult teaching from the Sermon on the Mount:

> Therefore everyone who hears these words of mine and puts them into practice is like a wise man who built his house on the rock. The rain came down, the streams rose, and the winds blew and beat against that house; yet it did not fall, because it had its foundation on the rock. But everyone who hears these words of mine and does not put them into practice is like a foolish man who built his house on sand. The rain came down, the streams rose, and the winds blew and beat against that house, and it fell with a great crash.
>
> When Jesus had finished saying these things, the crowds were amazed at his teaching, because he taught as one who had authority, and not as their teachers of the law. (Mt 7:24-29)

The way of Jesus is faithfulness. It is narrow, it bears good fruit, and it is on a solid foundation. Jesus wants our faithfulness, not our success. What if the church as we know it appears to be crumbling because we've built our house on sand? What if we've rooted ourselves in stories that offer weak nutrients and produce bitter fruit? What if this is an opportunity for us, dear church? The winds are indeed blowing and beating against the house, but the Bible reveals a story of grace, repentance, and new beginnings. I believe our story is far from over and that ultimately "the gates of hell will not prevail." I also believe that now is the time to *reclaim* the story that God has called us to live. It is scary to abandon so much of what we've always known, especially when it means that maybe we've gotten some things wrong. But the benefits far outweigh the cost.

Let us return to the radiant church Jesus calls us to be. A radiant church uproots itself from old, toxic, and tired narratives. A radiant church confuses those on the left and the right by rejecting dualism and embodying a politic not of this world. A radiant church abandons *me* for *us*, repents from the idol of success, and unhitches itself from inflexible partisan politics. A radiant church bears witness to the story rooted in the gospel. A radiant church has radiant people who tell—and live—the story of the gospel. As we do so, our imagination as a people opens up possibilities we never before dreamed of. May we be the church rooted in God's ultimate story of grace, lordship, redemption, and faithfulness.

QUESTIONS FOR INDIVIDUALS AND GROUPS

1. What stood out to you about the image of the sequoia tree? How does that relate to the environments we as the people of God root ourselves in?

2. What worldly or competing narratives form us away from God's radiant vision for the church?

3. In what ways has a sense of hyperindividualism harmed our witness?

4. What are key ingredients for the strength of our mission?

5. What is the purpose of the weekly worship gathering?

6. How does a church entrenched in partisan politics harm our witness?

7. What does it look like for the church to be engaged citizens without being entrenched in partisan politics?

8. What does it look like for the church to be rooted in God's ultimate story of grace, lordship, redemption, and faithfulness?

3

THE RADIANT VISION OF JESUS

WHEN I THINK OF MY GRANDMA JUDY, I think of Polaroid cameras. There was never a family gathering without multiple Polaroid moments. As a child it was so exciting and instant. She'd gather the family, tell us to say "cheese," and snap the picture. Anxiously, we'd wait several minutes for the picture to magically appear, and then Grandma would write on the white strip at the bottom of the picture the names of everyone in the picture, the occasion, and the date. Back then, it was magic. But when I compare the old Polaroid pictures to today's high definition photos, it doesn't seem so high-tech any longer. Polaroid pictures were always slightly distorted, and at times our faces would look slightly disfigured.

One of the most significant hindrances to the flourishing of the church in the West is our distorted pictures of God. Like the Polaroid pictures, there's enough distortion that the very character and heartbeat of God are disfigured.

Consider for a moment the various pictures of God you have internalized. Do you sometimes picture God as angry and waiting to lash out? Or is your picture of God a warm, fuzzy, Santa Claus figure applauding and approving your every move?

While these two pictures are rather polarizing, I have heard many well-meaning Christians describe both. Distorted pictures of God, however, aren't new. In the beginning, Satan worked hard to distort Adam and Eve's picture of God. When God told the first couple to not eat from the tree of the knowledge of good and evil, Satan distorted their picture of God into that of a liar. One of the first lies in the garden was that God cannot be trusted. Ever since, humans have had distorted and troubled pictures of God. Today, God is often viewed through brokenness, sin, idolatry, and bondage.

DISTORTED IMAGES OF GOD

Let's pull out a few Polaroids and consider the many distorted pictures of God we hang on our own refrigerators.

The distant god. The first Polaroid picture is one of a hardly visible god. God is unsympathetic, emotionally distant, and too busy to care about anyone's desires or needs. Often, when someone has this picture of God, they may be unmotivated to pray. And when they do pray, it often begins with something like, "God, if you can even hear me, . . . I know you're busy. . . ." Not only is God distant but is also too big to be known. God is too mysterious and too busy with important things to care about little ol' me. God is so vast and big that it would be impossible to even know God. Over time, the believer's heart becomes calloused, hardened toward this distant God after years of unanswered prayers or needs.

The punisher. As we look at the second Polaroid, we see lasers beaming from God's eyes and zeroing in on any poor sinner. We often hear about this god within harmful narratives from TV pastors after any major disaster. I once heard a celebrity pastor talk about a Lutheran church flattened by a tornado after its denomination voted to affirm same-sex marriage. This God-the-Punisher picture portrays a god who sends earthquakes, tsunamis, and tornados to regions, people groups, and nations who don't match that god's moral ideals. This god causes illness and disease and is an abusive bully ready to take down anyone who misbehaves.

The Santa Claus god. Look closely at Polaroid three and we see a jolly old man with a giant bag full of prosperity for all who know what lever to pull. Santa Claus god holds everything we could ever want or need to live our best life now. This god holds within his hands job promotions, mansions, luxury cars, opportunities galore, and all the desires of our heart. This god doesn't want us to sacrifice a thing, but instead to live in comfort, health, and wealth to our heart's content. All we need to do is know how to think, what and how to ask, and we'll get a generous bag of presents.

God the nationalist. In America, the fourth Polaroid has God holding an American flag in one hand and the Declaration of Independence in the other. God's purposes and plans are believed to be made manifest through this country's land, people, and borders. Anyone who stands against this nation's ideals also stands against God. God desires to bless America more than other nations, even to the detriment of other nations.

Ticket to heaven god. Shake the Polaroid for a moment and we see a god holding a golden ticket to heaven. Hell is a scary place, and often when we hear of it, we sigh in relief because we've been handed a ticket to heaven after praying the sinner's prayer. This picture of God has more to do with life after life on earth and a god who desires to rescue us from this awful place called earth.

"It's cool" god. In the sixth Polaroid, the god is likely slouching in a chair with a hat on sideways and two thumbs up. For this god, anything goes. God wants us to have our desires, so if it feels good, then it must be good. Eat, sleep, and live as you wish. Of course, the "It's cool" god has issues with other people's sins, but when it comes to our own, anything is good with him.

The party pooper god. I hate to say it, but in this Polaroid, God is sitting in a church pew with brows furrowed and arms crossed. This god doesn't like it when children laugh or run or play in church. Neither does he like it when the music is too loud or the art is too creative. Church is serious business, and anyone who has any fun is likely to be reprimanded by this god.

More than likely, we could pull out an entire album of Polaroid pictures of God. These distorted images of God can come from any of us, even deeply committed, well-meaning Christians. It's not uncommon for us to experience internal conflict about these pictures of God, anything from disturbing to fluffy. I'm not a psychologist; I like to leave that to my former colleague and pastor at PazNaz, Dr. Brad Strawn. He could tell us all about our primal wounds and how they shape our understanding of God. We develop these pictures due to various complexities and reasons, including abusive fathers, overbearing mothers, or anxious family members. But the implications are profoundly damaging to the fabric of our churches, and instead of a radiant witness, our witness is distorted.

Consider some of the implications for a moment. Whether we realize it or not, our pictures of God impact our worldviews, our lives, and how we view one another.

If God is distant, then we spend our entire lives feeling invisible, unloved, and unwanted by God. There would be little reason to engage with a god who doesn't engage with us anyway. Why pray? Why go to church? Why worship?

If God is a punisher, then we live with fear, shame, and a sense of failure. If God is a punisher, not only do we live in fear, shame, and failure, but we have a tendency to shame others. Further, when we live in fear of God punishing us, we're tempted to live dualistic and legalistic lives and expect others to do the same. Sadly, this has leaked into evangelism in some parts of the world. Evangelistic tracts depict God as angry and ready to punish people for their sins. Scaring people into confession, however, forms Christians who themselves view God as a punisher.

If God is Santa Claus, then we become angry and jaded when we don't get what we want. In turn we spend much time comparing our neighbors' possessions to ours. If God is Santa Claus, Christians become consumers, and the temptation is to find the correct buttons to push for prosperity.

If God is merely our ticket to heaven, there isn't much reason to live for God on earth—all that matters is the heavenly mansion prepared for us. The temptation is to disengage from the evil, brokenness, and oppression in this world.

If God is a nationalist, then anyone who isn't a citizen of that nation can be seen as an enemy and be treated as such. If God is a nationalist, then God favors only one nation and turns a blind eye to all others. If God is a nationalist, then the country's citizens supersede the people of God in Christ. The temptation is to reject all immigrants and embrace an elitist mentality.

Our pictures of God matter; they affect how we live and distort (or enhance) our witness. If the people of God are to be *imitators* of God, then our images of God matter all the more. What image of God are we imitating?

At the outset of John's Gospel, the apostle tells us that "No one has ever seen God, but the one and only Son, who is himself God and is in closest relationship with the Father, has made him known" (Jn 1:18). John is saying that the people of God didn't have a full and spectacular picture of God until Jesus came to earth. Before this, the revelation of God was limited. But when "the Word became flesh and made his dwelling among us," we for the first time "have seen his glory, the glory of the one and only Son, who came from the Father, full of grace and truth" (Jn 1:14). Now, there is no longer any reason to make our own personal constructs of God. There is no reason to take Polaroid pictures; rather, we have a picture of God standing right before us.

More than ever, the bride of Christ must courageously and vulnerably align itself with the one true picture of God. But where do we begin? With Jesus! Scripture tells us that Jesus is the One, the true picture of God.

In the Gospels, Jesus spends a lot of time revealing the character, nature, and heartbeat of God. When the disciples wanted a picture of God, Jesus emphatically reminded them in John 14:6-7, "I am the way and the truth and the life. No one comes to the Father except through me. If you really know me, you will know my Father as well. From now on, you do know him and have seen him."

Philip struggled with this. He couldn't comprehend it and wanted something more. But Jesus once again didn't pull out a Polaroid picture; he drew Philip's eyes back to himself as if to say, "Hello, Philip! Look no further. God is right here; look right here at me."

Jesus answered:

Don't you know me, Philip, even after I have been among you such a long time? Anyone who has seen me has seen the Father. How can you say, 'Show us the Father'? Don't you believe that I am in the Father, and that the Father is in me? The words I say to you I do not speak on my own authority. Rather, it is the Father, living in me, who is doing his work. Believe me when I say that I am in the Father and the Father is in me; or at least believe on the evidence of the works themselves. (Jn 14:9-11)

What is your picture of God? Look to Jesus. Jesus is

the image of the invisible God, the firstborn over all creation. For in him all things were created: things in heaven and on earth, visible and invisible, whether thrones or powers or rulers or authorities; all things have been created through him and for him. He is before all things, and in him all things hold together. And he is the head of the body, the church; he is the beginning and the firstborn from among the dead, so that in everything he might have the supremacy. For God was pleased to have all his fullness dwell in him, and through him to reconcile to himself all things, whether things on earth or things in heaven, by making peace through his blood, shed on the cross. (Col 1:15-20)

The author of Hebrews concurs: Jesus is "the radiance of God's glory and the exact representation of his being" (Heb 1:3).

A radiant church reflects the radiant image of God—Jesus. Jesus is the *radiance* of God's glory, and the church reflects the *radiance* of Jesus. The apostle Paul believed this to be true. He writes in 1 Corinthians,

Now the Lord is the Spirit, and where the Spirit of the Lord is, there is freedom. And we all, who with unveiled faces contemplate the Lord's glory, are being transformed into his image with ever-increasing glory, which comes from the Lord, who is the Spirit. (1 Cor 3:18)

Several chapters later Paul writes,

Just as we have borne the image of the earthly man, so shall we bear the image of the heavenly man. (1 Cor 15:49)

In Romans Paul writes,

Those God foreknew he also predestined to be conformed to the image of his Son, that he might be the firstborn among many brothers and sisters. (Rom 8:29)

And in Ephesians Paul implores,

Follow God's example, therefore, as dearly loved children and walk in the way of love, just as Christ loved us and gave himself up for us as a fragrant offering and sacrifice to God. (Eph 5:1-2)

Paul understands how awesome it is that the glory of God has been revealed in Christ. He understands that there was a time that humanity could not behold the full glory of God, but now the veil has been removed (2 Cor 3:16-18). Jesus is the clear, visible reflection of God. When we look to Jesus, there is no longer any question of who God is, and when we look to Jesus, we too are being transformed into the likeness of God.

Let's break this down.

LOOK TO THE CROSS

Many have wrestled with some portraits of God found in Scripture—that is, those portraits of a violent and vengeful God.

One time I had a conversation with someone at church who was struggling with these difficult images of God. Was God angry and waiting to lash out at any moment? Was God genocidal? These images can be profoundly oppressive for a Christian. I noticed this individual beginning to pull away from the church as his faith began to unravel. But when we look to the cross, things begin to change.

Greg Boyd says, "The cross is the supreme—indeed, the unsurpassable—revelation of God's loving nature. In all eternity, no event could ever reveal God's true self-sacrificial character more perfectly, for God could never go further for the sake of love than he went on Calvary."[1]

The cross—an upside-down display of power and "foolishness to those who are perishing" (1 Cor 1:18)—reveals the very nature and heart of God. At the cross we discover the self-sacrificial love, where the other-oriented character is on full display.[2] Greg Boyd says, "The love that characterizes God's eternal nature, and the love that his children are to extend to all others, *looks like the cross*. We might say that the cross is the definitive revelation of God's cross-like, or *cruciform*, character (emphasis added)."[3]

Our pictures of God matter. They shape our witness. If the people of God are to be *imitators* of God, then our images of God matter all the more. As we read through the Gospels, we discover that every Gospel account is headed to the cross. It's not just building in the event itself but in the teachings, miracles, and actions of Jesus. So by the time they arrive at the cross, the disciples begin to grapple with the teachings they had been wrestling with all along. Jesus' disciples now recognize the way of the cross all the way to the bitter end. As we build toward the cross, and as Jesus reveals the way of the cross through his teachings and actions, he pushes the disciples to go and do likewise. This is perhaps most highlighted in the "Way of the Cross Teachings" in the Gospel of Mark (see Mk 8–10). Jesus reveals that he must suffer; so must they. Jesus must lay down his life; so must they. Jesus must carry his cross; so must they.

We also see this type of modeling and commanding in John 13. On the same night Jesus would be betrayed, he gathered around the table with the disciples.

It was just before the Passover Festival. Jesus knew that the hour had come for him to leave this world and go to the Father. Having loved his own who were in the world, he loved them to the end.

The evening meal was in progress, and the devil had already prompted Judas, the son of Simon Iscariot, to betray Jesus. Jesus knew that the Father had put all things under his power, and that he had come from God and was returning to God; so he got up from the meal, took off his outer clothing, and wrapped a towel around his waist. After that, he poured water into a basin and began to wash his disciples' feet, drying them with the towel that was wrapped around him.

He came to Simon Peter, who said to him, "Lord, are you going to wash my feet?"

Jesus replied, "You do not realize now what I am doing, but later you will understand."

"No," said Peter, "you shall never wash my feet."

Jesus answered, "Unless I wash you, you have no part with me."

"Then, Lord," Simon Peter replied, "not just my feet but my hands and my head as well!"

Jesus answered, "Those who have had a bath need only to wash their feet; their whole body is clean. And you are clean, though not every one of you." For he knew who was going to betray him, and that was why he said not every one was clean.

When he had finished washing their feet, he put on his clothes and returned to his place. "Do you understand what I have done for you?" he asked them. "You call me 'Teacher' and 'Lord,' and rightly so, for that is what I am. Now that I, your Lord and Teacher, have washed your feet, you also should wash one another's feet. I have set you an example that you should do as I have done for you. Very truly I tell you, no servant is greater than his master, nor is a messenger greater than the one who sent him. Now that you know these things, you will be blessed if you do them. (Jn 13:1-17)

Jesus is modeling that the way of the cross isn't an abstract idea, but it's to be lived in community, usually counterculturally, and often uncomfortably. But Jesus calls his people to live this way, and it's the way he modeled.

A couple that I know—let's call them Joe and Jana—has taken this call rather seriously. Former Wall Street traders and bankers, they somehow stumbled across the book *The Irresistible Revolution* by Shane Claiborne. While reading it, Joe and Jana gave their lives to Jesus and understood that the way of Jesus is to live like Jesus. They left everything and moved to a marginalized community in Pasadena to simply be present among the people there. Many often want to know their plans, but for now they feel called to simply be present. Joe and Jana are often found hosting neighborhood dinners, standing on their lawns talking to neighbors, and even hosting the homeless in their home. More than once I've received a text like this: "Pray for us. It was raining and we felt led to open a bedroom to one of our friends who is homeless." Their hearts are big, their imaginations may seem reckless to some, but they are living in the way of Jesus. They are constantly reminding me that the way of imitating Jesus doesn't always add up or make sense, and oftentimes people may shake their heads at the perceived recklessness, but it seems to me the way of Jesus *is* seemingly reckless, just like the cross.

When our vision of Jesus is in line with the Scripture's vision, it alters and disrupts our lives. Like Paul's encounter on the road to Damascus, the scales on our eyes begin to fall away, and we learn to see that the way of Jesus is the way of the cross and often is drastically different from our distorted images of God. It matters who we are imitating.

Who are we progressing toward—Christlikeness or our falsely constructed distorted gods? Who are we reflecting? When the world looks at the bride of Christ, do they see the loving God or one of hate? Do they see the generous God or a selfish one? Do they see the gracious God or a merciless one? Do they see our kind God or mean one? Do they see a peacemaking God or a warrior god?

BEHOLD THE RADIANT IMAGE OF JESUS

When I behold Jesus as revealed in Scripture, our worldly constructs begin to melt away. Instead of the nationalist god, at the cross we see that national boundaries are obliterated, and in Christ we are one. Instead of an angry judge, we see the loving God who offers *himself* to the sinner. Instead of a warrior god, we see the God who turns the other cheek in the face of violence. Instead of a distant god, we discover the God who moves *toward* the rejected, forgotten, marginalized, invisible, and sinful. Instead of an elitist god, we see the God who stoops low, chooses downward social mobility, and takes on the cup of suffering. Instead of a partisan-politics god, we discover the God who doesn't fit into worldly ideologies and instead calls us to be citizens of a different kind of kingdom—one where political parties mean *nothing* and the way of Jesus as Lord is *everything*.

When we truly behold the radiant image of Jesus, we are transformed into his radiant image. Behold, dear church. Let us behold the one and true image of God—Jesus. Let us fall in love with the Jesus of Scripture. Let us be a people who saturate in the Gospels, memorize the teachings of Jesus, and align ourselves with the way of the cross.

IMAGINE A CHURCH IN THE RADIANT IMAGE OF JESUS

Please don't conclude that my proposition in this chapter is *just live like Jesus*. There is nothing simple about learning, knowing, and living the ways of Jesus. But perhaps we can begin with what is considered the *greatest* way to live as Jesus did.

In the Gospel of Mark, Jesus gives us the Great Commandment:

One of the teachers of the law came and heard them debating. Noticing that Jesus had given them a good answer, he asked him, "Of all the commandments, which is the most important?"

"The most important one," answered Jesus, "is this: 'Hear, O Israel: The Lord our God, the Lord is one. Love the Lord your God with all your heart and with all your soul and with all your mind and with all your strength.' The second is this: 'Love your neighbor as yourself.' There is no commandment greater than these." (Mk 12:28-31)

We can reflect the heart of Jesus by way of living out the Great Commandment: love God with everything and love our neighbor as ourselves. Jesus not only teaches this but lives it out by caring for those in the ditch, by healing on the Sabbath, by healing the blind, by washing the disciples' feet, by the bitter moment at the cross. Radiant churches reflect the radiant image of Jesus by living out Jesus' Great Commandment.

When COVID-19 first rocked the world, pastors were trying to navigate pastoring churches through a pandemic. While gathering as the church is a central call for the people of God, pastors and churches were also forced to ask, "What does it mean to be the church without buildings and programs? What does it look like to reflect the radiant image of Jesus when the Sunday morning gathering is no longer the main thing?" Not only was it an innovative time for churches and pastors, but it was an opportunity for us to reflect the image of Jesus as not just a gathered people but also a scattered and sent people. Of course, for many who are missionally minded—like Joe and Jana—this is no problem. But for some, Sunday morning had become the main event. So what do we do when the main event is taken away?

At PazNaz, while we were still worshiping via our livestream ministry, we saw this as a moment for us to reflect the bright and radiant image of Jesus by living out the Great Commandment in our community. Though we couldn't gather in person, our city still allowed us to care for our community through our Helping Hands Ministry and Church in the Park Ministry. Before COVID-19, our Helping Hands Ministry, a food bank, fed around 250 people a week. Our Church in the Park Ministry feeds roughly 100 homeless individuals a hot breakfast every Sunday morning.

The good people of PazNaz chose love instead of fear, generosity instead of hoarding, and compassion instead of ignoring others. It was beautiful to watch our people reflect the radiant image of Jesus every week. By the fourth week of COVID-19, our church was feeding roughly 1,300 people in our Helping Hands Ministry, and they continued to faithfully cook hot burritos and prepare a full breakfast for the homeless every Sunday morning beginning at 6. Watching countless people selflessly show up wearing masks, gloves, and staying physically distanced from one another out of love looked a lot like Jesus. I *saw* the radiant image of Jesus in our people.

Every week, the realities of COVID-19 presented restrictions, barriers, and new problems, but every week, I watched our people lean into God's imagination and overcome difficulties and serve our community. PazNaz radiated the image of the invisible God through COVID-19.

Imagine the witness of the church that looks more like Jesus and less like political leaders of the day. Imagine a church that says "you first" instead of "me first." Imagine a church that defies cultural norms for the sake of others. Imagine a church that goes out of its way to care for the stranger in the ditch. Imagine a church that lays down its resources for the sake of the community. Imagine a church that exists not just for itself but for the world. Imagine a church that imitates Jesus, looks like Jesus, and lives like Jesus. I imagine this church, and it's a church I yearn to participate in.

QUESTIONS FOR INDIVIDUALS AND GROUPS

1. What are some of the distorted images of God you've carried with you throughout your faith walk?

2. Of the distorted images the author describes, which ones have shaped you the most?

3. When you look to Jesus, how does this change your picture of God?

4. If the cross is the ultimate picture of Jesus, how does that shape the call of the Christ-follower?

5. List five ways Jesus is radiant. How does this bring you hope and encouragement?

6. List five ways the church can be radiant. How does this bring you hope and encouragement?

4

THE RADIANT KING
AND KINGDOM

WHEN WE BEGIN TO TALK ABOUT THE KINGDOM, some might think of heaven—that is, a place where we all get to go someday. Heaven will indeed be radiant. The vision of the radiant heaven has brought me much comfort whenever a loved one or a dear saint in our congregation dies. Knowing that someday these tired bodies of ours will be resurrected, and we will join with the redeemed creation in the new heaven and new earth is an invigorating hope. As Paul says, "Where, O death, is your victory? Where, O death, where is your sting?" (1 Cor 15:55).

At times, however, I am concerned by evangelicals' propensity to focus on heaven as *someday far away* instead of *right here, right now*. A future-only focus on heaven, I fear, can create a heavenless people here and now. Not only that, but has our obsession with a future-only heaven impacted our discipleship, evangelism, and theology? Does our obsession with a future-only heaven cause us to focus on getting a ticket to heaven instead of on our role as citizens in God's heaven or *kingdom* on earth?

John F. Kennedy said, "Ask not what your country can do for you—ask what you can do for your country." This famous quote propelled Americans to think differently about their role as citizens in this country. Instead of thinking about what the government or its leaders can do for the citizens, the citizens were forced to consider *their role* in creating a better country.

It has been said that if we simply ask better questions, we will get better answers. At times, I wonder if our obsession with a future-only heaven has caused us to ask weak questions.

HOW DO I GET TO HEAVEN?

"How do I get to heaven?" has been a leading question for evangelicals for several decades. When I was a teenager, I was deeply concerned about this question.

I'll never forget sitting in a Hardee's on a dreary January morning. I was what I'd call a "seeker" at the time. There were many stirrings and longings in my heart to experience something real and beautiful, and the witness of the students in my high school who walked with Jesus was attractive. There was something about them—a way—that led me to believe there was something about this Jesus they spoke of. So I started attending a local Campus Life group. After my first visit, two of the leaders invited me to meet them for breakfast at Hardee's the next day.

It was a miracle that I made it to breakfast at 7 a.m. as a teenager. I nervously walked in, yet I was excited to hear more about Jesus. The breakfast began with the two leaders asking me a series of questions about my family, my favorite food, and my hobbies. As our time together came to a close, they asked me one last question: "Tara Beth, let's just say you walk out of Hardee's today and get hit by a bus and consequently die. And then let's say you were to stand before the pearly gates of heaven, face-to-face with Jesus. How would you respond if Jesus were to say to you, 'Tara Beth, why should I let you into my perfect, sinless heaven?'"

I don't remember all that I said that morning, but I do remember awkwardly picking at my egg sandwich for a bit and then saying, "Well, I clean my room when my mom tells me to, and I've never been arrested."

Of course, the leaders were fishing for a very particular answer. It was a common 1990s evangelism tactic that would lead unsaved "sinners" to consider how they might get into heaven. I thought about it. The picture of hell seemed terrifying, and I definitely didn't want to go there. But I went to the breakfast, interestingly, to hear about Jesus. I wanted to know *who* this Jesus was, I wanted to know *what* Jesus thought of me, and I wanted to know *what this meant* for my life.

Christians have had an obsession with heaven, and that's not bad. I myself enjoyed working with Scot McKnight as an assistant when he wrote his book *The Heaven Promise!* We like to speculate what heaven will be like: Who will be there? Where will we live? Will we sleep? How do I get there? We speculate who will be there and who won't. So we wonder, *How do we get there?*

ASKING BETTER QUESTIONS

I believe our focus on a future-only heaven has caused us to ask weak questions. We are starting at the wrong place. What if getting to heaven and escaping the bad place isn't all there is to the Christian life?

In the Gospels, Jesus doesn't talk much about a future-only heaven. Similarly, there isn't much discussion about how to get into a future-only heaven. Instead, Jesus proclaims *who he is* and the type of life he wants his disciples to live *on earth*. In the Gospel of Mark, Jesus does a lot of this. He proclaims who he is as Messiah, and then he tells the disciples what kind of life they ought to live on earth:

> He then began to teach them that the Son of Man must suffer many things and be rejected by the elders, the chief priests and the teachers of the law, and that he must be killed and after three days rise again. He spoke plainly about this, and Peter took him aside and began to rebuke him. (Mk 8:31-32)

Jesus continues,

> Then he called the crowd to him along with his disciples and said: "Whoever wants to be my disciple must deny themselves and take up their cross and follow me. For whoever wants to save their life will lose it, but whoever loses their life for me and for the gospel will save it. What good is it for someone to gain the whole world, yet forfeit their soul? Or what can anyone give in exchange for their soul? If anyone is ashamed of me and my words in this adulterous and sinful generation, the Son of Man will be ashamed of them when he comes in his Father's glory with the holy angels." (Mk 8:34-38)

And later he says,

> You know that those who are regarded as rulers of the Gentiles lord it over them, and their high officials exercise

authority over them. Not so with you. Instead, whoever wants to become great among you must be your servant, and whoever wants to be first must be slave of all. For even the Son of Man did not come to be served, but to serve, and to give his life as a ransom for many. (Mk 10:42-45)

Over and over, Jesus reveals what kind of Messiah he is, what kind of death he will die, and how the disciples then are expected to live as his followers. Jesus couldn't have been any clearer or any more repetitive. Jesus will suffer and carry his cross, and to be a follower of Jesus likewise means suffering and carrying one's cross.

And yet the disciples kept pressing in with really bad questions. "What must I do to be first? Who gets to sit at your right hand in the kingdom? Who will be the greatest?" These remind me of some of the questions Christians ask today: How can I get to heaven?

The disciples were clearly missing the point. Jesus was flipping their worldview on its head. To be a follower of Jesus means living like Jesus—and it wasn't easy or glamorous. To be a follower of Jesus isn't about getting to heaven or being first in the kingdom or even about being greatest in the kingdom. Instead, the life of discipleship looks a lot like Jesus' life. The life of discipleship isn't focused on getting into a future-only heaven, but it is about following the radiant King, being a radiant people, and living on earth as it is in God's radiant kingdom.

KING JESUS, OUR RADIANT KING

But there's more. There was something *exceedingly special* about him. Jesus was born in a quiet, forgotten, and marginalized place of society. Nevertheless, he was *special*. He was the long-expected Messiah and King. He was fully human—he breathed, walked, felt pain, and laughed—that is, he understood the *fullness* of the human experience. And he was also divine. Yes, flesh but fully divine.

He was the one the people of God had waited for, ached for, yearned for, and prayed for. His own mother's prophecy reflected this longing:

> My soul glorifies the Lord
>> and my spirit rejoices in God my Savior,
> for he has been mindful
>> of the humble state of his servant.
> From now on all generations will call me blessed,
>> for the Mighty One has done great things for me—
>> holy is his name.
> His mercy extends to those who fear him,
>> from generation to generation.
> He has performed mighty deeds with his arm;
>> he has scattered those who are proud in their inmost
>>> thoughts.
> He has brought down rulers from their thrones
>> but has lifted up the humble.
> He has filled the hungry with good things
>> but has sent the rich away empty.
> He has helped his servant Israel,
>> remembering to be merciful
> to Abraham and his descendants forever,
>> just as he promised our ancestors. (Lk 1:46-55)

His teachings were different, fresh, and new. He crossed cultural boundaries and loved indiscriminately. He loved those who were *off-limits* to the religious elites. He healed the sick, restored the sight of the blind, and forgave the extreme sinner.

Let's return to Mary's prophecy of her royal son. Read it again, but slowly, and take note of the nature of the kingdom.

First, the faithfulness of God toward Israel. God has remembered God's people. While God's people were hard-hearted, God was soft-hearted. When God's people were rebellious, God was merciful. When God's people were bruised, battered, and abandoned, God *moved in*.

Second, Mary prophesies that this king—yes, her son—would inaugurate an upside-down kingdom. For the poor, this was great news. At last their bellies would be filled, and those who held power over them would be sent away empty-handed. This was *disturbing* news to the wealthy and powerful. But there's something stunning about this announcement that can't be diminished: there wasn't anything worldly or normal about this King.

This upside-down kingdom would be inaugurated through the meekness of a child, not through rebellion or war. And the new world order doesn't necessarily support the status quo, nor does it necessarily support the worldview of the rich and powerful. This is good news for the poor, the lowly, the humble, the weary, the hurting, the persecuted, and those who call on the name of the Lord. It is good news for those who recognize that without the God of Israel, there is no other way. It is good news for those who are desperate for this King and his upside-down kingdom, and nothing else.

In other words, this is good news for the broken, not for those who say "I've got this." This is good news for the sick, not for those who say "I know how to help myself." It is good news for the humble, not for the proud. For the oppressed, not for the oppressor. For the excluded, not for the excluder. For the suffering, not for the self-sufficient and powerful. For the desperate, not for those who trust in their own power. For those who cry out, "God, I need you!" not for those who say, "Life is just fine without you." It is good news for those who say, "Without you I am nothing!" but not for those who say, "All that I have is everything." Mary understood fully the gravity of this good news she would bear. She knew it in the aches of her bones and her belly; she would give birth to a King who would inaugurate a very special and subversive kingdom. He would be no ordinary King, but a radiant one.

Third, the life, teachings, and character of Jesus make Mary's revelation credible, which should blow our minds! Many parents rub their pregnant bellies trying to guess what kind of child they will raise. "Will she be the next Einstein?" "Will she be like her daddy?" "Will he be a pro baseball player like his grandfather?" Maybe some parents get it right, but I'd suspect their guesses are child's play compared to Mary's proclamation of Jesus. The pages of the Gospels reveal that her prophetic words about Jesus were accurate.

Jesus begins his ministry with echoes of Mary's words:

Jesus returned to Galilee in the power of the Spirit, and news about him spread through the whole countryside. He was teaching in their synagogues, and everyone praised him.

He went to Nazareth, where he had been brought up, and on the Sabbath day he went into the synagogue, as was his custom. He stood up to read, and the scroll of the prophet Isaiah was handed to him. Unrolling it, he found the place where it is written:

"The Spirit of the Lord is on me,
    because he has anointed me
    to proclaim good news to the poor.

> He has sent me to proclaim freedom for the prisoners
>> and recovery of sight for the blind,
> to set the oppressed free,
>> to proclaim the year of the Lord's favor."

Then he rolled up the scroll, gave it back to the attendant and sat down. The eyes of everyone in the synagogue were fastened on him. He began by saying to them, "Today this scripture is fulfilled in your hearing." (Lk 4:14-21)

Jesus begins by declaring that he is the Anointed One, and he follows it up with revealing the nature of this upside-down kingdom. Jesus came to proclaim good news to the poor, freedom for the incarcerated, healing for the blind, and to set the oppressed free. Much like Mary's proclamation, this is *great news for the forgotten, the poor, the oppressed, the invisible, and the marginalized.* This is not your normal king.

The life, teachings, and death of Jesus were not normal either. He pushed the boundaries of the religious conservatives by rubbing shoulders with the unclean and notorious sinner. He taught in ways that caused the experts of the law to tilt their heads and furrow their brows. He broke spoken *and* unspoken rules. Eventually, it got him killed.

His royal coronation made no sense to the disciples. Even though Jesus told them he would suffer and die, they could not and would not accept that. So when Jesus rode into Jerusalem on his donkey, I wonder, when the disciples heard the crowds cry out, "Hosanna!" whether they suddenly erased all of Jesus' way-of-the-cross teachings from their memories. Perhaps they thought Jesus had been delusional, but now they will get the king they want. Except, there were some things about that day that still were *off.*

There was no warhorse, just a borrowed donkey. There were no fine garments thrown on the streets, just tattered clothing from the bottom of society. There was no great war or rebellion, just a peaceful Messiah who said that in the kingdom, we turn the other cheek.

This feeling of something being *off* continued when Jesus was put on trial by the chief priests and religious leaders. Again, what kind of king is put on trial? *Shouldn't the rebellion begin* right *about now?* his followers wondered. Isn't this the time when Jesus overthrows the rich, powerful, and oppressor? But he didn't. He turned the other cheek as he was whipped, spat on, mocked, and ridiculed. He turned the other cheek when a crown of thorns was pressed into his skull and nails were driven through his hands. He turned the other cheek as his chest caved in and he cried out, "Father forgive them, they know not what they do!" He turned the other cheek as he submitted, "Father, into your hands I commit my Spirit!" As he took his last breath and cried out, "It is finished," the earth shook, the seas roared, and the mountains trembled.

And then it was over.

Or was it? His coronation wasn't typical by any means. It definitely wasn't what the disciples expected of their King. They wanted splendor, power, force, and might. Naturally, they wanted the Roman Empire to be overthrown and for the Jewish people to enjoy privilege and favor once again. His teachings were confusing and odd, so the disciples seemed to have selective hearing. At the culmination of the crucifixion, the disciples believed Jesus' movement was at the bitter end.

But then, just days later, the earth trembled again and the seas roared in praise. Turned out, not a thing could keep Jesus in that tomb—not sin, not death, not Satan, and not his adversaries.

Jesus was not dead, but alive! Jesus appeared to disciples outside of the tomb, around dinner tables, on dusty roads, and on fishing boats. He continued teaching them that he was the fulfillment of God's plan from the beginning, and he continued painting his vision of this upside-down kingdom.

The royal carpet was rolled out, and the train of his robe filled the world with his glory as he ascended to the throne where he now reigns today and forever.

Let that soak in for a moment.

Jesus is King.

The King is among us.

This is everything.

Jesus is the radiant King who came to establish the radiant kingdom on earth and has called his citizens to be radiant people. Have we as Christians gotten all wrapped up in the wrong emphases? Jesus taught us to pray in the Lord's Prayer:

Your kingdom come,
your will be done,
    on earth as it is in heaven. (Mt 6:10)

Our call as God's radiant people isn't to figure out what to do to get into the future heaven but instead to live like the King's radiant kingdom citizens and witness to God's radiant kingdom on earth.

ASKING BETTER QUESTIONS

Maybe the questions we ask should be different. What if Jesus' way isn't about "getting saved to get into heaven"? Maybe the question we ought to lean into is *If Jesus is King, then how should we live?*

I often wonder if our obsession with getting into a future-only heaven has caused us to worry less about living faithfully in the kingdom and being God's radiant people on earth. I wonder what kind of Spirit-filled revival would break loose in the North American church if we pressed in and wrestled more with this question, *If Jesus is King, then how should we live as kingdom citizens?*

I believe most would answer the question this way: If Jesus is King, then those who live in the kingdom ought to live as the King calls us to live—that is, as citizens of his radiant kingdom. Radiant kingdom citizens live under the King's reign and live as the King asks us to live. Citizens of the kingdom look a lot like the King—loving, kind, selfless, and cruciform. When Jesus calls us to "be perfect" as the "heavenly Father is perfect" (Mt 5:48), he is calling us to live and love as the Father and Son live and love.

Further, Paul implores the people of God to "be imitators of God" (1 Thess 2:14). We orient ourselves by the things the King is oriented toward. We lay down our lives just as the King laid down his life. We love those the King loves. We pursue those the King pursues—that is, we pursue the lost, broken, and hurting. We love them and lift them up, just as the King does. We show them the same hospitality Jesus shows. If Jesus is King, we ought to look and act like him.

My husband, Jeff, is quite the Mr. Fix It and is often seen with a tool in his hand. He rarely hires anyone to do anything. It took nearly nine years of marriage before Jeff allowed anyone other than himself to change the oil in one of our cars.

So when Caleb, our oldest son, was born, he watched his daddy fix everything. Caleb often follows his daddy around the house with a toy hammer or screwdriver, mimicking Jeff. Not too long ago, Jeff was working underneath a car, so Caleb ran inside to grab his toolbox and began fixing his fire truck. Jeff decided to play along and prop up the fire truck for Caleb to get underneath.

Caleb follows in the footsteps of his daddy so much that he is becoming just like his dad. I watch Caleb's mannerisms, phrases, and actions and think, *Wow, that is just like Jeff.* Now, both of our boys imitate their father on a regular basis.

Whether Jeff was under the sink, on a ladder, raking the leaves, mowing the lawn, repairing the car, or wielding a hammer, the boys wanted to do what Jeff was doing. They wanted to be just like their daddy. The big idea? We imitate who or what we love and revere. The apostle Paul admonishes us to "be imitators of God, as beloved children; and walk in love, just as Christ also loved you and gave Himself up for us, an offering and a sacrifice to God as a fragrant aroma" (Eph 5:1 NASB).

A strange thing begins to happen when we spend a significant amount of time around someone—especially when we admire them. We start to sound like them, act like them, and live like them. As citizens of the King's radiant kingdom *on earth*, we are called to participate with God as God builds God's radiant kingdom by imitation of and participation with the King.

PARTICIPATION WITH THE KING

When I was a teenager, Jesus absolutely *saved* me. I am confident that someday my broken body will be made new in the resurrection, and someday I will be a citizen of the new heaven and new earth. Jesus *saved* me as a teenager and continues to save me, but Jesus also calls me to more. Jesus calls me to *participate* with him. In other words, I don't admire Jesus from a distance, and he isn't a feel-good friend that I reach out to now and then. And my love for him isn't merely an intellectual thing. All of God's people are invited to participate in the divine life. Michael Gorman describes the life of participation with Christ:

The mode by which salvation is conveyed to the world is the preaching of this good news both in word and deed. And the mode by which that salvation is received is best described not as faith in the sense of intellectual assent but as faith in the sense of full participation, a comprehensive transformation of conviction, character, and communal affiliation. This is what it means to be "in Christ."[1]

As kingdom citizens who live under the reign and rule of King Jesus, we are to imitate the King and are called to participate with the King. Believing that King Jesus is at work in our world, kingdom citizens are called to partner and colabor in redeeming all of creation. We do this by living and loving as the King, which we do by participation. We participate in the life of Christ when we feed the hungry, visit the incarcerated, welcome the immigrant and orphan, give generously, welcome our neighbors to our table, work to dismantle systems of oppression, and serve our community. God is at work redeeming all of creation, and our call is to partner with God in this work.

For Jeff and me, participation has led us around the country and eventually to Pasadena. Moving to Pasadena wasn't a career move for us. For that matter, it wasn't a great career move for Jeff. Jeff was, at the time, climbing the ladder at his dream job as an engineer at Northrop Grumman. When we sensed the Spirit calling us to Pasadena, Jeff had no job lined up. When he sat down with his manager at Northrop Grumman, he asked Jeff what company he was going to next. Jeff didn't have an answer. His manager, coworkers, friends, and some family members thought Jeff was crazy to leave a job that many young engineers would love to have. But for us it was never about a career move. We believed God was calling us to participate in the work of the kingdom in Pasadena. For our family, serving the church in Pasadena was an act of participation with the King, and it was an act of obedience.

For citizens of the King's radiant kingdom, participation *here and now* matters. We are called to be colaborers and partners with the King as the King builds a radiant kingdom here and now.

OBEDIENCE TO THE KING

King Jesus calls us to obedience, responsiveness to his calling, and participation in the work that he is doing around the world. And it is a narrow road, as Jesus tells us in the Sermon on the Mount.

When I lived in Southern California, I had a lovely book on the history of Southern California. I used to flip through it on a lazy day and read about the history of where I lived. In it are beautiful pictures that gave me a portrait of the San Gabriel Valley down throughout the decades. I loved scrolling through and staring at the photos. Each page gave me a beautiful snapshot and portrait of life in Southern California. Scot McKnight says that "the Sermon on the Mount is the moral portrait of Jesus' own people."[2] When we read the Sermon on the Mount, we get a fuller vision of what it looks like to live in the already-but-not-yet kingdom of God. When we read the Sermon, we see what it means to be the people of God in every century.

Jesus' words are at times uncomfortable. Sometimes when we read the Sermon, we attempt to tone it down. We like to pick what we think we ought to abide by, and usually we pick the teachings we think *others* ought to abide.

But there's something particularly special about Jesus' Sermon on the Mount. It is for those who are truly *all in* for the Christian life. I mean, we can't read the Sermon on the Mount and be *somewhat* in. We simply can't tone it down or soften it. Jesus asks for all: our obedience, our minds, our hearts, our bodies, our emotions, our character, our decisions, our finances, our talents, and our relationships—all with him at the center as our guide and authority.

Jesus closes the (uncomfortable) Sermon with his parable of building one's house on rock rather than sand. And the people were amazed with his teaching (Mt 8:1).

Jesus closes his sermon with a powerful image of two kinds of people. Some will hear Jesus' words and water them down—they are the ones who build the house on sand. Others who hear Jesus' words fall to their knees, turn their lives around (repent), and go all in for the Christian life. Though the words of Jesus are difficult, they obey, lean in, and follow. They are so captivated by Jesus' vision for the Christian life that they leave everything to follow him, know him, and imitate him. On this particular day, many who heard this sermon were amazed and followed him. Will we do the same?

Is Jesus the ultimate authority of your life? Jesus sets himself up as the decision-maker, the authority, the ruler, and the king for all Christians. Are you leaning in to his authority?

In 2010 I began my seminary journey with Northern Theological Seminary. I had studied Bible in undergrad and had been in full-time pastoral ministry for six years, but I knew it was time to go back to school. With a nine-month-old at home and another child on the way, my goal was to simply get through school—to survive. I'll confess; my attitude wasn't the greatest. I had already been a student of the Bible, I had ministry experience, but I wanted the degree. I approached my first few classes with a bit of arrogance and impatience. I would hurry in and hurry out of each class without truly soaking in the words of my professors. My first summer at Northern, I enrolled in a week-long module on the book of Revelation taught by Gerald Borchert. When I walked into the class and sat down, and a seventy-eight-year-old man slowly walked into the room and sat down, I slumped down into my chair and thought to myself, *This is going to be a long and boring week; bring on the caffeine.*

Dr. Borchert sat down, opened his Bible, and began to read the opening words to the book of Revelation and the vision of Christ so majestically illustrated by John. And then he began to teach in a way that I had never before experienced. His words were penetrating, convicting, and authoritative; eight hours of teaching evaporated in a moment. Next day, I ran to the first row of the classroom and sat on the edge of my chair while hanging on to every word he had to say. For the first time at Northern, I took on the posture of a student. I cared about every word Dr. Borchert had to say and was hungry for more. I was open to learning new things, and, most of all, I allowed the words to form my heart, mind, and soul.

Jesus calls all Christians to be humble, open, and surrendered students absorbing and obeying the teachings of Jesus. Jesus calls us to participate as kingdom citizens. What is our posture to the teaching and lordship of Jesus? Are we eager students ready to walk in the footsteps of our Lord? Jesus, the radiant King, calls his radiant people to participate in the radiant kingdom on earth as it is in heaven by *doing what the king asks of us.*

GOD'S RADIANT KINGDOM ON EARTH AS IT IS IN HEAVEN

In the early 2000s a group of lay leaders from PazNaz saw the significant homeless crisis in the city. Pasadena is beautiful and affluent. It is also a city where marginalized people groups barely get by, including folks who end up homeless for a variety of complex reasons. When God's radiant people take the King's radiant teachings seriously, their hearts break for the things the King's heart breaks for and do something about it. Radiant kingdom citizens take seriously the prayer, "thy kingdom come on earth as it is in heaven," and work to build God's radiant kingdom here and now. When the group of lay leaders saw the homeless crisis, their hearts broke.

They began to act on this problem by showing up on Sunday mornings in Pasadena's Central Park. Each week these radiant lay leaders were showing the hope and love of Jesus with their presence and a box of donuts. Eventually, the donuts turned into a hot breakfast, including oatmeal, juice, coffee, pastries, and breakfast burritos. Then the radiant people decided to expand the feeding program and offer a worship service with music and preaching. Tables and chairs were added so the homeless could sit at a table instead of on the grass. The PazNaz people learned their newfound friends' names, built relationships, and heard their stories. Now, some of the radiant people from PazNaz have committed to be with our homeless friends for the long haul.

For over twenty years now, God's radiant people at PazNaz have not missed the opportunity to serve and show the love of Jesus to the people in Central Park. Rain or shine, hot or cold, storm, Christmas, Easter, there they are. Today, dozens upon dozens of volunteers wake up at the crack of dawn to make a hot breakfast, load up a truck and trailer, and unload a truck and trailer to set up a sound system, tables, chairs, and a hot buffet. There, Jesus is proclaimed, and relationships are built. Why? Because our radiant King tells us that when we feed the hungry, we feed him. Because when we believe God's will is to be done on earth as it is in heaven, we believe in restoring a broken and hungry world on earth. Jesus is a radiant *King* and asks his radiant *people* to build a radiant *kingdom* here and now.

Let's circle back to *the* question Christians ought to frame their lives: *If Jesus is King, then how should I live?* We are called to be citizens of God's radiant kingdom on earth as it is in heaven by living like the King, participation in the life of the King, and obedience to the King. When we live like the King, we take our cues from the King. We take his teachings seriously. The people in the kingdom live as the King lives. The people of the kingdom are oriented toward the things the King is oriented toward. We lay down our lives just as the King laid down his life. This, you see, is how the radiant King calls his radiant kingdom citizens to live *on earth as it is in heaven.*

QUESTIONS FOR INDIVIDUALS AND GROUPS

1. When you imagine heaven, what do you imagine?

2. What are the problems of an overemphasis on a "future-only heaven"?

3. Imagine heaven on earth here and now. What would it look like in its fullness?

4. What does it look like for the church to live this out on earth?

5. How does reframing our question from "How do I get to heaven?" to "If Jesus is King, then how shall I live?" impact discipleship?

6. If Jesus is King, then how should the church live in today's world in the King's way?

5

THE RADIANT WITNESS

I AM NOT A SPORTS ENTHUSIAST. If I attend any sort of sporting event, I go for the food and pay attention for the first thirty minutes—if I'm lucky. Super Bowl events are all about the commercials and buffalo wings dip. I could hardly tell you how most sports work.

I grew up in a baseball family. By "baseball family" I mean every weekend baseball was on the television (mainly the Chicago Cubs). My grandfather was a professional baseball player, and my dad published a book about baseball. Most Sunday afternoons I would fall asleep on the couch while Dad watched a game on TV. To this day, whenever I hear a baseball game in the background, I suddenly get in the mood for a nap. But although I grew up in a baseball family, I was *not* a baseball person. And that would be an understatement. Congregants squirm when I use a sports illustration in a sermon because I will inevitably say something incorrect.

There were exceptions to my sports enthusiasm, however. Whenever my hometown Chicago teams were doing well, I paid attention. In the 1990s, it was exciting to watch the Bulls, and I'll never forget the excitement during the Bulls' two three-peats. There was a time or two when the Bears were getting close to winning the Super Bowl, so I paid close attention then. I watched the Blackhawks when they were playing for the Stanley Cup. You might say then, "You're a fair-weather fan!" I'm not sure you could even call it that. I'm more of an occasional wannabe sports fan. Here's the thing. I am only attracted to sports when things get exciting. I want to be a part of the excitement, celebrations, and energy.

The Cubs won the World Series the year my family moved to California. As it was building to the final game, I grew increasingly homesick. My social media news feeds were filled with the excitement of friends celebrating on the streets. Watching some of the videos, I was overcome by the emotion of it all. Complete strangers were hugging and crying in the streets, and thousands of the fans surrounded Wrigley Field singing songs, dancing, and celebrating. I wanted to be there with all of them. Suddenly, I wanted to be a sports fan.

Watching the celebrations all the way from California drew me in. There was such a beautiful sense of shared joy, togetherness, and hope. The Cubs fans drew me in. When I saw them singing in unity in front of Wrigley Field, I wanted to be right there singing with them. When they talked about hope, I wanted to taste the hope they had held onto for 108 years. When I saw strangers hugging and crying, I cried and wanted to experience the same shared excitement and joy. When I saw the fans in the streets throughout the night in a euphoric celebration, I felt like I was missing out.

Can you imagine if the church had that kind of effect? What if those who don't consider themselves to be all that into church are suddenly drawn in by the people who call themselves the church? What if those on the outside looking in see something so attractive, so beautiful, and so radiant that they can't help but *want* to be a part of it? When the church is singing a melody of love and hope, imagine those watching from afar respond, "We're missing out on something beautiful." When strangers become family and share the same hope of the kingdom, imagine outsiders saying, "I want that."

I believe the church has something to offer that the world *doesn't have*. I believe this from the depths of my soul. Not because we as a people are so great and such do-gooders—sadly, all too often we are far from that!—but because Jesus' kingdom is coming and is readily available to all who gather for the feast. When we gather *in his name*, strangers have something to celebrate, enemies are reconciled, and celebrations last into the night because God's team wins. If we get this right, those watching from a distance will fear missing out; they will be drawn in, captivated, and attracted to the kingdom readily available to all.

You see, this is the central vision of Scripture. God's people are called to live in such a way that the world is blessed through us—through our actions, our life together, and our love. At the heart of God's grand narrative in Scripture is not merely the story of individuals being rescued so they can avoid the bad place but rather a holy and radiant people. That is, we—the church—are to display a better way of living, a fresh way of living, a stunning way of living, and a radiant way of living to a weary and broken world.

The source of this radiance, however, is found in the one and only King Jesus—*he is the radiant source*. In Christ, that radiance bursts out of our worship, our relationships, and our work in the world. It isn't just our deeds that attract outsiders but Jesus himself in us.

THE OUTSIDERS FROM THE EAST

In a stunning story found in Matthew's Gospel, Jesus is the radiant light that draws those outside of God's people—the magi from the East. Likely Zoroastrian priests from Persia, the wise men possibly knew very little about Israel's longings for a Messiah. These peculiar men would have been experts in the occult, astronomy, astrology, but not Jewish history. They represented pagans, Gentiles, and outsiders, not God's chosen people. They weren't well versed in Jewish Scriptures, they didn't have the longings of the Jewish people, and yet something drew them in—something *radiant*. The bright star had such a grip on their imaginations that they were willing to make a thousand-plus-mile journey to catch a glimpse of what it foretold. They traveled with gold, frankincense, and myrrh.

Getting lost in Jerusalem, they wanted to know where to find this King. Somehow, they knew that this King was different from what they experienced in the capital city. Somehow, they knew that King Herod represented worldly superpowers and not the King they were looking for. It was as if they knew this King was different from any king they had known.

Consider the juxtaposition for a moment. King Herod, a representative of the Roman Empire, powerful and grand, and King Jesus, small, meek, and unknown. Born at the margins, humble, not glamorous, with no military ribbons. However, the one born at the margins attracts the outsiders from the East. One king made grand entrances; the other's entrance was humble. And yet it was Jesus who attracted the wise men from the East, not Herod.

Not the one hitched to the worldly superpowers. Jesus is, after all, the *radiant one.*

John 1:5 tells us, "The light shines in the darkness, and the darkness has not overcome it." And Jesus later proclaims, "I am the light of the world. Whoever follows me will never walk in darkness, but will have the light of life" (Jn 8:12). And in John's first epistle, he echoes Jesus' words, "This is the message we have heard from him and declare to you: God is light; in him there is no darkness at all. If we claim to have fellowship with him and yet walk in the darkness, we lie and do not live out the truth. But if we walk in the light, as he is in the light, we have fellowship with one another, and the blood of Jesus, his Son, purifies us from all sin" (1 Jn 1:5-7).

Jesus is *the* radiant light that shines bright in a dark and weary world. Our calling as a radiant people, bearing witness to a radiant king, cannot and will not happen apart from the radiant King.

God has chosen us—the church—to bear witness to this radiant King. But are we bearing witness in such a way that we are actually attracting "wise men from the East"? And if I can bring it a step further, which king do the wise men from the East see us imitating? The worldly superpowers, or the humble one born in the manger?

As a pastor, I care very much about our witness. To bear witness to the good gospel takes courage for churches. While the gospel subverts the status quo and shames the worldly powers, it is radiant and attractive to the poor, hungry, and hurting.

RADIANT CHRISTIANS IN LOVE AND SOLIDARITY

In 2016, within my first few months of pastoring at PazNaz, I was faced with shepherding a church through significant polarizing issues, including a presidential election and back-to-back police shootings of two Black men—Philando Castile in Falcon Heights, Minnesota, and Alton Sterling in Baton Rouge, Louisiana. Following these all-too-common incidents, five police officers were killed by a sniper in the middle of what was supposed to be a peaceful rally protesting the shootings of Philando Castile and Alton Sterling. These shootings were tragic no matter which way you looked at them, but they were also symptomatic of hundreds of years of systemic racism in this country. I've since learned that polarization is the new mode of operation for White evangelicals, but as a thirty-four-year-old pastor, this was new territory.

Many took sides—"Blue Lives Matter!" "Black Lives Matter!" It was a racially charged time across the United States. Around the same time, there was another incident of police brutality in Pasadena. Pastorally, I knew I couldn't step into the pulpit and simply continue on as if nothing had happened. I wanted nothing more than for the people at PazNaz to be a radiant light amid so much pain, hate, fear, and racism. I saw this dark and polarized time as an opportunity for us.

On Friday, July 8, 2016, I received a call from Kerwin Manning, who pastors a large and historic Black church in Pasadena. I had grown to love and deeply respect Kerwin. He is a pastor of pastors and a community organizer. Together we lamented the brokenness and pain in our nation and city. He then said to me, "Now, Pastor Tara Beth, we need you."

"Anything, Pastor. What do you need?"

He said, "I want us pastors to organize a citywide prayer vigil in downtown Pasadena this Sunday night on the steps of city hall. I want your church to come, and I need you to get them there. Can you do that?"

Gulp.

It wasn't that I didn't want to be there. I just knew what I'd be up against as a new, young female pastor. You see, that same time and same night was the PazNaz's annual choir concert called the Favorites Concert. Every year, the choir and orchestra came together to perform all their favorite songs of the year. This is followed by an ice cream social on the patio. This event was a *big deal* for our church, and I didn't know if I had the capital to not only cancel such a beloved event but to also ask our church to join something that was so polarizing. However, I knew we had to be there. I knew there would be loss, but there was too much at stake for us to *not* be there on the steps of city hall.

"Kerwin, we will be there." I hung up the phone and panic set in.

One by one I called our pastoral staff and told them about this decision, which no doubt was top-down. Some were confused, some were upset, and some were excited. I sent an email out to the church, hit up social media, and made an announcement from the pulpit. As I expected, some were livid that I would make such a call. But I wanted our church to bear witness to a good and radiant gospel of peace, love, solidarity, and reconciliation. We had to be there.

I'll never forget stepping up on the steps of Pasadena's city hall and overlooking the crowd of several thousand people. Like a child looking for their parents at a choir performance, I scanned the crowd for my people. As I did, I lost count. Hundreds from PazNaz were scattered throughout the crowd. There they were, standing in solidarity, ready to pray, ready to listen, and ready to be a radiant light in our city. I couldn't believe it.

While our nation was hurling epithets, engaging in social media wars, and choosing physical and verbal violence, the churches of Pasadena gathered to peacefully pray. One by one, pastors got behind the microphone and prophesied, lamented, proclaimed, and prayed. For several hours the churches of Pasadena stayed, prayed, lamented, and stood in solidarity. That night, I saw a radiant church in Pasadena. That night, I saw Jesus, the gospel, hope.

A month later I met a new woman in our church. When I asked her what drew her to PazNaz, she said it was our church's presence in Pasadena. "I knew this was a church that cared about racial injustice in our world, and I knew that this was a church I wanted to be a part of."

WHAT KIND OF PREVIEW ARE WE GIVING?

My family is weird. We like to show up to movies on time so we can catch the previews. Growing up, I thought movie previews were sometimes the best part of the show! The previews give us a glimpse into what's to come; they give insight into the story being told. Producers know that the one-minute movie preview is *critical*. Within one minute or less, the viewer often decides whether or not to see the movie being previewed. When theaters started previewing the newest *The Lion King* movie, I watched it from my computer at home. Thank goodness! I was in a pool of tears within seconds. The movie preview had that kind of grip on me, and I knew I had to see it.

Whether we like it or not, we have been chosen to give the world a preview of God's very good kingdom. Sometimes, it seems, we are giving a preview of the wrong kingdom. Are we giving the wise men from the East a preview of a church that tears down families? Are we giving the world a preview of a wealthy group that ignores the voices of the marginalized? Are we giving them a preview of Christians who turn a blind eye on the moral bankruptcy of our own people? Are we giving them a preview of leaders who misuse and abuse power? Are we giving them a preview of a kingdom that applauds the voices of the superpowers and cast asides the meek? C. S. Lewis said, "When we Christians behave badly or fail to behave well, we are making Christianity unbelievable to the outside world."[1]

Whenever I make decisions that subvert the powers of misogyny, sexism, or racism, I see spiritual powers rear their wild and ugly heads. During the COVID-19 pandemic, when churches were navigating whether or not to reopen after President Trump declared all churches to be "essential," the leadership at PazNaz began to discern whether it was time to open the campus. I saw this as an opportunity to lovingly shepherd the people through a greater imagination of what it means to be the church—that is, without access to the church campus and without access to the familiar programs. While gathering is central to what it means to be the people of God, it's also essential that we practice Jesus' Great Commandment of loving our neighbor. They will know we are Christians by our *love and care for our neighborhoods.* The PazNaz pastoral leadership knew it was unwise to open the campus and also not loving. As with most pastors, after the announcement that we would not be opening the campus, the emails started pouring in. I'll never forget one in particular:

> These reasons for not reopening are not good enough. Get it together, man. You have had time to organize your own version of plans that will satisfy governmental requirements. You don't need an offering plate. You can improvise something. . . . A drop off box or SOMETHING! This is just another bad decision influenced by your WOMAN

head pastor. Women head pastors are not Scriptural. I don't care what you say about it. I have studied the issue. Do you go by what the Bible says OR do you go by what is politically correct?

This email—although coming from one individual—is again symptomatic of the misogyny, contempt, bitterness, and hatred that has fueled far too many evangelicals for too long. Emails like this are far too common, and although I'd like to chalk it up as "crazy," I actually think this is one aspect of the spiritual warfare we face, and sadly, this is the witness many display across White evangelicalism.

It's a tale of two previews: one of love, solidarity, peace, and another of misogyny, bitterness, and contempt. I want to pastor a church that displays to the world a bright and radiant gospel, not one of misogyny, bitterness, and discord. Dear Christian, what kind of preview are we giving the world?

A RADIANT CHURCH PREVIEWS THE FUTURE

Revelation 21 describes the new heaven and new earth as a glorious place, which I look forward to. But it's not only something to wait for and look forward to, but we are to embrace that vision and allow it to impinge on the present. In part, the apostle John tells us of his heavenly vision:

Then I saw "a new heaven and a new earth," for the first heaven and the first earth had passed away, and there was no longer any sea. I saw the Holy City, the new Jerusalem, coming down out of heaven from God, prepared as a bride beautifully dressed for her husband. And I heard a loud voice from the throne saying, "Look! God's dwelling place is now among the people, and he will dwell with them. They will be his people, and God himself will be with them and be their God. 'He will wipe every tear from their eyes. There will be no more death or mourning or crying or pain, for the old order of things has passed away. (Rev 21:1-4)

Someday, there will be a world of *no mores*. That is, there will be no more racism, no more sorrow, no more oppression, no more misogyny, no more injustice, no more polarization, no more hatred, no more antagonisms. But as sons and daughters of the resurrection, this hope we look forward to isn't a someday only-future hope, but we look to the future to cast a shadow on the present. Radiant churches and radiant people wed themselves to this vision. Radiant churches look to Revelation 21 and say, "If someday there will be *no more racism*, then we will work to create spaces of reconciliation and healing now." Radiant churches say, "If someday there will be *no more misogyny*, then we will work to heal gender inequality and promote equality within the church." Radiant churches say, "If someday there will be *no more injustice*, then we will partner with God in the work of bringing peace and justice on earth as it is in heaven."

A radiant church looks to the promises in Revelation 21 and doesn't sit back and wait for that to come. Instead, the church grabs hold of it in the power of the resurrection and previews to a weary world the ways of hope, healing, and life.

A RADIANT CHURCH PREVIEWS MERCY

Most churches in America want to attract the outside world for all the right reasons. But sometimes our attempts are shallow and lacking. The church in North America is working almost too hard to attract the world through tactics similar to those the world is using. Certainly, I'm not throwing the baby out with the bath-water. The creative and innovative ways I see churches attract outsiders through creative worship are incredible, and I thank God for the ways God is reaching people through these means. We are a gathered people—the *ekklēsia*—and when we are empowered by the Holy Spirit in our gathering, our gifts of creativity are magnified.

At the same time, I wonder if we are too often putting the "emphasis on the wrong syl-la-blé." That is, are we putting an emphasis on attracting our neighbors through glitzy worship services, killer music, lights, fog machines, outstanding programs, and good preaching, but forgetting about our very ordinary—yet weird—call to offer something the world *can't* offer? It was these ordinary yet weird acts that flipped the Roman Empire on its head. Mike Frost puts it this way:

> While evangelists and apologists such as Peter and Paul were proclaiming the gospel and defending its integrity in an era of polytheism and pagan superstition, hundreds of thousands of ordinary believers were infiltrating every part of society and living the kind of questionable lives that evoked curiosity about the Christian message. They surprised the empire with their unlikely lifestyle. . . . These ordinary believers devoted themselves to acts of kindness. They loved their enemies and forgave their persecutors. They cared for the poor and fed the hungry. In the brutality of life under Roman rule, they were the most stunningly different people anyone had ever seen.[2]

The mission of God, in which we are invited to participate, is perhaps simpler yet more stunning than what many of us fail to realize. There is so much pain, darkness, and brokenness in this world, and our call as Christians isn't to "build it so they will come" but to flip the world on its head through *ordinary* acts of love, mercy, and generosity.

WHEN THOUGHTS AND PRAYERS AREN'T ENOUGH

Several years ago I watched a friend, let's call him James, write about his financial, emotional, and spiritual struggles on Facebook. He was once a pastor who lost his job, was going through a divorce, and was barely making ends meet financially. Every week, almost daily, he transparently shared his struggles, and the comment section would be full of words of encouragement:

- I'm praying for you!
- I believe in you!
- God's got this!
- God is on the throne!
- God is with you.
- Praying for you constantly, brother.

One day he wrote a very raw and honest response. James shared, "I'm tired of hearing that people are praying for me. I don't feel any less alone, and I already know that God is with me. But I'm barely making it financially anymore, and I'm not even sure if I can put food on the table this week. Frankly, I need help." Of course, his comment section was fairly empty. It dawned on me, however, that thoughts and prayers weren't enough. James needed something more. Jeff and I got in touch with him and wire transferred him some money so he could get groceries. I don't share this to make you think Jeff and I are some kind of heroes. We're not. But I did learn a lesson that day—sometimes "thoughts and prayers" just doesn't cut it.

There's a lot of tragedy, pain, and need in this world, and at times it gets overwhelming. Sometimes the easiest responses are to turn a blind eye altogether. We are a stressed out and maxed out world, and so many of us feel as if we have our own lives to take care of. So sometimes, the easiest thing to say is, "I'm praying for you." When we say that, let's make sure we are actually praying for the person, and let's also ask the Lord what an act of mercy might look like for them.

I wonder if we are sometimes missing the point altogether. I imagine one of my children being in need, for example. What if one day when my boys finally have their driver's license, one of them—let's say, Caleb—ends up in a ditch with a flat tire? Then, my other boy, Noah, drives up next to his brother and says, "What's wrong, Caleb? Why are you in the ditch?" Then Caleb explains that he has a flat tire and asks Noah if he would help with the flat. Instead, Noah, who has everything needed to help Caleb, says, "I'm so sorry. Thoughts and prayers. I'll let Dad know of your need," and abruptly drives away. As their mama, this would grieve my heart. I would *hope* that instead of this happening, Noah would get out of the car and help his brother change the flat tire.

Hang with me here. In his Beatitudes, Jesus said, "Blessed are the merciful, for they will be shown mercy." I believe this is perhaps one of the more important concepts for Christians living in North America. We have forgotten what it means to be merciful.

Too often we correlate mercy with being nice. In the Beatitudes, however, Jesus was working off of an Old Testament or Hebrew understanding of mercy—that is, mercy is something one *does*. Mercy is freeing the oppressed, feeding the hungry, providing hospitality to the traveler, caring for the poor, and clothing the naked. The prophet Isaiah says,

Is not this the kind of fasting I have chosen:
to loose the chains of injustice
    and untie the cords of the yoke,
to set the oppressed free
    and break every yoke?
Is it not to share your food with the hungry
    and to provide the poor wanderer with shelter—
when you see the naked, to clothe them,
    and not to turn away from your own flesh and blood?
Then your light will break forth like the dawn,
    and your healing will quickly appear;
then your righteousness will go before you,
    and the glory of the LORD will be your rear guard.
Then you will call, and the LORD will answer;
    you will cry for help, and he will say: Here am I.
     (Isaiah 58:6-9)

Mercy is something *one does*, and acts of mercy are almost always *inconvenient*. Being merciful is almost always an interruption. It almost always required Jesus to stop what he was doing, go out of his way, give up time, give up energy, and give up emotion. Over and over, Jesus was stopped *in his tracks* by those crying out for deliverance. In Matthew 9, 15, 17, and 20, for example, as Jesus was traveling, those in need cried out to him, "Have mercy on me!" Every single one of these cries came from those who were in some kind of bondage. None of them could help themselves. They were stuck, they had big needs, and they needed *someone else* to deliver them. So they cried out to Jesus in utter desperation, and we see Jesus respond to cries of mercy by healing the lame, feeding the hungry, forgiving sins, caring for the sick, and setting those free who are in bondage.

Glen Stassen calls mercy "compassion in action."[3] Mercy is the act of *partnering with God* in delivering someone from their need. Time and again, as Jesus traveled and was stopped in his tracks, he revealed compassion *in action by delivering others from the bondage of need.* Never once did Jesus say, "I'll pray for you." Not once. Now, I don't think we should stop saying that; sometimes it is one of the most meaningful things we can say to someone.

Prayer is an act of love, but if it keeps us from acts of mercy, are we truly praying? Again, we must pray for people. But when it becomes an alternative to mercy, we are missing the blessing altogether.

Jesus' brother James gets at this as well:

> What good is it, my brothers and sisters, if someone claims to have faith but has no deeds? Can such faith save them? Suppose a brother or a sister is without clothes and daily food. If one of you says to them, "Go in peace; keep warm and well fed," but does nothing about their physical needs, what good is it? In the same way, faith by itself, if it is not accompanied by action, is dead.
>
> But someone will say, "You have faith; I have deeds."
>
> Show me your faith without deeds, and I will show you my faith by my deeds. You believe that there is one God. Good! Even the demons believe that—and shudder. (Jas 2:14-19)

James understood that faith without *mercy* is dead. This may very well sound like works righteousness. Scot McKnight clears this up for us, "To the merciful is promised divine mercy at the judgment, that is, entrance into the kingdom. While this blessing creates a disturbance for us at times about works righteousness, its design is to remind us that mercy is fundamental to a proper love of God and others."[4] In other words, acts of mercy are utterly central to what it means to live out the Great Commandment, *love God and neighbor*. Mercy is a natural outflow of one who loves God and neighbor.

There is a lot of brokenness, bondage, decay, and need in this world. What if "thoughts and prayers" are only part of the equation? Historian Rodney Stark says a leading factor caused the Jesus movement to light up the world—mercy. He writes,

> In the midst of the squalor, misery, illness, and anonymity of ancient cities, Christianity provided an island of mercy and security.... It started with Jesus.... In contrast, in the pagan world, and especially among the philosophers, mercy was regarded as a character defect and pity as a pathological emotion: because mercy involves providing *unearned* help or relief, it is contrary to justice.[5]

Consider that for just a moment. Let that sink in. Mercy changed the world. In the middle of squalor and misery, mercy lit the Roman world on fire. Today, squalor, misery, and illness surround us, and God chooses *us* to partner together in setting the world right through everyday ordinary acts of mercy.

I yearn for the church to be known not for glitzy programs, awesome music, and entertaining preaching. Instead, I want to be a part of a church that is an *island of mercy* in a world full of misery.

A RADIANT CHURCH

Peace Lutheran Church was located in a struggling neighborhood in Lauderdale, Minnesota. The neighborhood church was once described as a nonentity, dark, with little goodwill.[6] Though it was once near death, it quadrupled its membership by the most unexpected means. Peace Lutheran Church says it is "open to everyone," but it doesn't expect people to come to them. They go to their neighbors through radiant acts of mercy. Instead of working to attract the neighborhood by good coffee on Sunday morning or innovative worship and preaching, they decided to be the church by *doing* mercy.

They canvassed their neighborhood with seven hundred fliers offering roofing, plumbing, and repair—all free of charge. An article in *City Pages* says, "The idea was to deliver neighbors from the duress of big-ticket bills, the kind that leaves families punished by debt, or unable to pay at all."[7] At first, Peace Lutheran had few takers, but they continued to clean homes, build chair lifts, repair roofs, and paint siding. There were no strings attached and no requirement to come to church. Peace Lutheran just wanted to love their neighborhood through ordinary acts of mercy. Eventually, word spread, and more people were calling out to the church to be released from bondage. The church always showed up with compassion in action.

Peace Lutheran Church's membership has quadrupled, not by a bigger building, more programs, and better preaching but by the most beautiful yet ordinary means. The seeds of the gospel are sown in these ordinary acts of mercy. May we, the church, be an island of mercy in a world full of squalor, misery, and illness.

A RADIANT GENTLENESS

Living as an attractive community that bears witness to the radiant gospel means living as a community in contrast to the world of strife, decay, and brokenness. But when I scroll through my newsfeed, I see Christians mimicking the ways of this world through divisive and even hateful tactics. Where's the contrast?

Not too long ago I was scrolling through my newsfeed and noticed an article posted about a young man who attacked and killed a World War II veteran. The story is atrocious, vile, and gut-wrenching. But as I read the response of my Facebook friend who posted the article, I was appalled. His response is graphic and may be triggering for some. In short it was a horrific description of what this person would like to do to the young man who took the life of the World War II veteran.

Sadly, responses like this are not at all uncommon these days. Often, when something evil, unjust, or oppressive happens, we see responses like "I'll show them," or we fight back or say harmful, hateful, and violent words. Sadly, throughout history, Christians sometimes resolve conflict with more conflict or violence or force or manipulation or coercion. When someone offends us, we gossip and use dehumanizing words about them. When someone wrongs us on the road, we respond with road rage. If someone says something we disagree with, we resort to name-calling. When conflict happens in a local church, it often produces divisive chatter and gossip. If someone does something we don't like, we exclude them from the table.

Furthermore, when something happens in the public square that Christians aren't keen on, we fight, get angry, shout, protest, and use dehumanizing words and names. After all, we "simply can't allow this to happen; we can't sit on our hands and do nothing!"

I contend, however, that we too often have anemic imaginations on how to handle conflict. Our thinking is often too binary: we choose violence, gossip, and rage, or we do *nothing* at all. We want the extremes.

Jesus stepped into a similar context. Israel wanted a king who would overthrow Rome with force and violence. They wanted the chariots and swords; they wanted a king who would rule with an iron fist. Israel (including the disciples) could imagine no other alternatives. Instead, they got a king who rode into the city on a donkey, and his royal coronation was a crown of thorns. Jesus stepped into a polarizing and binary context and proclaimed alternatives. He showed a third way. He lived a radical alternative.

In Jesus' Beatitudes, he spoke of people who choose a third way of living. "Blessed are the meek," he said, "for they will inherit the earth" (Mt 5:5). When we think of the word *meek*, we picture someone who is unable to speak up for themselves. A meek person is usually seen as the invisible one in the corner who hides in the face of injustice. Meekness is often understood as the antithesis of loud, strong, and power. However, this common understanding could not be any further from the heart of this beatitude.

The Greek word for *meek* in the New Testament can be defined as gentleness or a strength that is under control. In this text, Jesus is speaking to people stuck in an unjust situation. They are suffering but choose not to seek revenge. These people are poor and are stuck in a system with no clear path out. They have suffered under the hand of violence over and over again. These people are insulted unjustly. They have been rejected, forsaken, and abandoned. These people have been left in the ditch with no one to care for them.

Today, the meek are those who have been unjustly demoted, overlooked, forgotten, and excluded from the table. Though they are kind, they have been stabbed in the back, treated poorly, and ignored. They have gifts and talents but are constantly overlooked and rejected. They feel invisible in a room full of power brokers and ignored by those with important titles.

Instead of using force to remedy the injustices they face, they renounce violent, coercive, and forceful methods. Consider the subversive nature of this text. Jesus promises that they will inherit *land*. When I was in grade-school history class, I learned how people acquired land: by war, weapons, and power. But Jesus flips this upside down and advocates a new path. Instead of fighting, Jesus calls for gentleness. In the kingdom, land is inherited, not by worldly tactics, not by force, not by violence, but by gentleness.

Instead of responding to injustice with violence, the people Jesus speaks of remain meek. Mousey? No, meek. A doormat? No, meek. An enabler? No, meek. Invisible? No, meek. Watch the world go to hell in a handbasket? No, meek. Turn a blind eye? No, meek. Jesus consistently portrays the kingdom vision for God's people as a living alternative in a world gone awry.

In a polarized world full of antagonism, Christians often have no imagination for alternatives. We either sit back and do nothing, or we fight back. We're either passive or aggressive; turn a blind eye or respond with an iron fist. Jesus steps into this context and teaches a different way:

> You have heard that it was said to the people long ago, "You shall not murder, and anyone who murders will be subject to judgment." But I tell you that anyone who is angry with a brother or sister will be subject to judgment. Again, anyone who says to a brother or sister, "Raca," is answerable to the court. And anyone who says, "You fool!" will be in danger of the fire of hell.

> Therefore, if you are offering your gift at the altar and there remember that your brother or sister has something against you, leave your gift there in front of the altar. First go and be reconciled to them; then come and offer your gift. (Mt 5:21-24)

Later Jesus says,

> You have heard that it was said, "Eye for eye, and tooth for tooth." But I tell you, do not resist an evil person. If anyone slaps you on the right cheek, turn to them the other cheek also. And if anyone wants to sue you and take your shirt, hand over your coat as well. If anyone forces you to go one mile, go with them two miles. (Mt 5:38-41)

And he continues:

> You have heard that it was said, "Love your neighbor and hate your enemy." But I tell you, love your enemies and pray for those who persecute you, that you may be children of your Father in heaven. He causes his sun to rise on the evil and the good, and sends rain on the righteous and the unrighteous. If you love those who love you, what reward will you get? Are not even the tax collectors doing that? (Mt 5:43-46)

Jesus doesn't just teach these alternatives; he embodies them. For example, as the cross was looming, Jesus was taken away by authorities. One of Jesus' disciples, Peter, takes matters into his own hands and attacks one of the men with the Jewish authorities, slicing off his ear. One can hardly blame him. Peter saw an unjust situation and responded. But Jesus powerfully steps in and says, "No more of this!" and heals the man's ear (Jn 18:10-11).

Jesus shows us a better way. He shows us the way of peacemaking, love, gentleness, healing, and reconciliation. However, we too often don't have an imagination for Jesus' way. It's either this or that; one extreme or the other. We, the very people of God who are connected to the imagination of the artist of the universe, can do better. As the people of God in Christ, instead of embracing binaries of the world, our call is to find alternative paths— paths that embody the way of Jesus, the way of love. When we do this, we sing a melody that is not of this world and a harmony that emboldens a new imagination for living.

BOLD REPENTANCE

The absolute antithesis to God's vision for the church is a dark church of strife, division, and brokenness. Where there is division, our call is to partner with God to bring peace and shalom; where there is decay, our call is to partner with God to plant seeds for new life; where there is hatred, our call is to participate in the work of peacemaking; where there is racism, our call is to bring healing and reconciliation. Which preview will we give the world? One that is attractive, bright, and illuminating? Or will we preview division, misogyny, racism, contempt, and hatred?

Perhaps it's time to repent. Repentance isn't just feeling sorry for our ways but an active turning away from sin and evil and walking in God's brilliant light. To be a bright witness, we must name our sin, confess where we've fallen short, turn away from our old ways, and allow the future hope to impinge on the present. A radiant church is a repenting church.

QUESTIONS FOR INDIVIDUALS AND GROUPS

1. Has there ever been a group of people that you have been attracted to simply because of their enthusiasm, unity, or joy?

2. Think about a time the church attracted "outsiders" because of the enthusiasm, unity, and joy within the body.

3. Think about a time the church turned away "outsiders," perhaps because of the lack of enthusiasm, unity, and joy within the body.

4. If the church is a preview to God's kingdom, what kind of preview are we giving?

5. Why aren't "thoughts and prayers" always enough?

6. Could the church be better at being merciful?

7. What does a meek church look like?

6

THE RADIANT PARTNERSHIP

IT WASN'T LONG AFTER GIVING MY LIFE to Jesus that the Lord gripped my heart and imagination for ministry. All I wanted to do was preach, so I preached anywhere I could—I preached in front of mirrors, to my youngest brother, to the cornfields, and in my front yard. I was enamored of Billy Graham for his effectiveness in preaching. I too wanted to proclaim the gospel in such a way that it drew others to love Jesus.

However, within a short time of being called to ministry, my Youth for Christ director made it clear that I couldn't be a pastor, I couldn't preach to adults, and I couldn't preach on a Sunday morning—ever. I was devastated but accepted that theology because I wanted to please God. *I'll marry a pastor*, I thought. *Then I can be in ministry, minister to people, and join my husband in his calling.*

Well, I didn't marry a pastor. I married a rocket scientist instead. And I've come a long way since then. But this long journey hasn't been smooth. (I share more of my story in my earlier book *Emboldened*.)

When I was installed as the new senior pastor at PazNaz, there was one major controversy: gender. I've worked hard to remember my main call is to be a local church pastor, not an activist for women in ministry. In fact, I have never preached a case for women in ministry from the pulpit at PazNaz. My heart beats for Jesus and his church on mission in a weary world. While I didn't go into ministry to talk about women in ministry, it is a conversation that we must steward well. Why? Not because I'm for women and against men, not because I'm angry and resent my brothers in ministry, and not because I desire women to take over the church. I think this conversation matters because of Jesus, the gospel, and the mission of God.

Since writing *Emboldened*, almost weekly I have received letters from women around the world who are ready to walk away from ministry altogether. Fighting toxic forms of patriarchy and searching for a place at the table are exhausting.

Sadly, women do walk away from the church. Gifted, talented, and godly women become repulsed by the blatant rejection they experience. When the church holds women back, we suffer. We are missing out.

"Laurel" is a pastor in central Ohio. She was so excited when her district leader received her résumé and called her to learn more about what kind of church she wanted to pastor. Although the denomination Laurel serves affirms women, not many churches call women to be their senior pastor. The district leader told her, "I have to be honest. Your résumé is great, but there aren't many churches in my district who will call a woman." But still, Laurel was hopeful. Her résumé was beautiful. She was at the top of her class in seminary, she won an award for excellence in preaching, and she is influential among her peers.

Yet when it came to finding a church to serve, days turned into months and months turned into years. Laurel eventually realized that it "wasn't worth the battle" and took her gifts to corporate America, where she is thriving vocationally. "I still have dreams of using my gifts for the church someday," she bemoaned, "but I'm too tired now to fight that battle."

As a female pastor, I find stories like this gut-wrenching. I often wonder how much more our light would shine with brilliance if gifted women were welcomed to the table like our gifted brothers. I've often wondered, *How many women with incredible gifts for the kingdom are tragically unaware of their gifts because they have no imagination for their role in the church because they've never seen anyone like them?*

Dear church, we are missing half of the team for this mission we've been invited into. In a radiant church, men *and women* come to the table with the same goal, vision, and mission. In a radiant church, all hands are ready to serve, ready to use their gifts, and ready to be on mission together.

There is, no doubt, tension between men and women in the world, and it's tragic that this exists in the church. We see this tension heightened in movements such as #MeToo and #ChurchToo. These are hard conversations that cause people to raise their defenses and antagonisms flare. Post anything on Twitter about gender roles in the church, and the trolls come out. This isn't just a women's rights issue, a justice issue, or a gender issue. It's a gospel issue and a missional issue. Perhaps to better understand, we need to go back to the beginning of the story— that is, the story that ultimately reaches its pinnacle in *Jesus*.

GOD'S IDEAL FOR MAN AND WOMAN

In the beginning, God created a beautifully diverse, complex, and interwoven tapestry, which included the dirt we stand on, the mountains we climb, and the oceans we surf. It also included a diverse humanity of many races, cultures, contexts, and a man and woman. When creating this grand tapestry, God said,

> "Let us make mankind in our image, in our likeness, so that they may rule over the fish in the sea and the birds in the sky, over the livestock and all the wild animals, and over all the creatures that move along the ground."

> So God created mankind in his own image,
>> in the image of God he created them;
>> male and female he created them. (Gen 1:26-27)

What is often missed here is the radical nature of this account. God created both male *and* female in God's image. There is no less-than party in view here, and there is an assumption of equality. In a world where men held the power, Genesis was written in a way that reveals God's heartbeat for male and female—both are created equally in the image of God. Not only that but Adam and Eve were then invited to rule the earth *together*. It does not say man will rule and Eve will support his ruling. Instead, they will rule together. Carolyn Custis James makes an important observation about God's calling Adam and Eve:

> He is not simply saying "both" male and female have callings, but their calling is one. He is making a rather shocking countercultural point that his sons need their ezer-warrior sisters to become the men God created them to be and to

fulfill their purpose in this world. This won't happen if they move forward without God's daughters. "It is not good for the man to be alone."[1]

When God created Adam, "The LORD God said, 'It is not good for man to be alone. I will make a helper suitable for him'" (Gen 2:18). When many read this passage, subordination is read into the text. Naturally, when we think of a "helper," we think of a hierarchy with men at the top and women secondary. Many who subscribe to complementarian theology look to this passage as the backdrop for the case that God created a hierarchy of man and woman. At first glance it makes sense. But when we get into the original language, the word for "helper" is *ezer*. "The LORD God said, 'It is not good for man to be alone. I will make a helper [*ezer*] suitable for him.'" But let's first take a look at how this word is used in other Old Testament Scriptures:

There is no one like the God of Jeshurun,
  who rides across the heavens to help you
  and on the clouds in his majesty. (Deut 33:26)

Blessed are you, Israel!
  Who is like you,
  a people saved by the LORD?
He is your shield and helper
  and your glorious sword.
Your enemies will cower before you,
  and you will tread on their heights. (Deut 33:29)

We wait in hope for the LORD;
  he is our help and our shield. (Ps 33:20)

I lift up my eyes to the mountains—
  where does my help come from?

> My help comes from the LORD,
> the Maker of heaven and earth. (Ps 121:1-2)

These are powerful passages that have been recited by the people of God for centuries. Indeed, God is our *helper*! Does this then mean God is subordinate? I should think not.

Furthermore, *ezer*, notes Carolyn Custis James, is a term often used in military contexts.[2] When God's people are fleeing from their enemies or marginalized from a worldly superpower, the people of God call on their God to rescue them from the hands of their oppressor. Consider the implications for a moment. Eve—*ezer* (Gen 2:18)—is a fierce *warrior* who participates in the strenuous work of the kingdom, on the front lines. This battle, which is not of flesh and blood, summons *men* and *women* to battle the forces of evil in this world, proclaim the power of the gospel, and participate in the work of setting the captives free from the evil oppressors of this world.

In Genesis 2:23, Adam says, "This [woman] is now bone of my bones and flesh of my flesh," which is a way of saying, "This is me, just in a different form." The implications here are complementing equality and uniqueness within togetherness. Adam and Eve together create something uniquely beautiful, mysteriously one, and perfectly complementing each other. Carolyn Custis James notes,

> Far from polarizing male and female—as patriarchal defini-
> tions do—or highlighting gender distinctions between
> them . . . God's method in creating the woman unites them
> in bone level solidarity. When the man sees the woman, he
> doesn't distinguish himself from her. He sees a reflection of
> himself. She is literally bone of his bones and flesh of his
> flesh, perfectly reengineered into a woman. The oneness

between God's male and female image bearers is unmistakable and utterly profound.[3]

One thing seems clear: there is no subordination at play. They are one, and their calling, ruling, and living are as one. This was God's original intention. But today, men and women are at odds. What went wrong? Sin, rebellion, and curses entered the scene. Everything crumbled rather abruptly.

The slithering serpent salesman entered into the scene, and God's vision for man and woman as one collapsed when Eve and Adam rebelled. Not only is humanity's relationship with God fractured, but there is a crevasse between man and woman. God's perfect shalom is destroyed on earth, and the unity Adam and Eve once had now put them at odds. This is reflected in the curses of Genesis.

God declared the curses and says to Eve, "Your desire will be for your husband, and he will rule over you" (Gen 3:16). When I was young, I interpreted the word *desire* as a sense of longing. Especially when I was a teenager and had dreamy ideas of marriage, *longing* for my future husband made a lot of sense. However, this is the same word used in Genesis 4:7 when Cain was swimming in anger, bitterness, malice, and rage toward his own brother, Abel. God found Cain and said, "Why are you angry? Why is your face downcast? If you do what is right, will you not be accepted? But if you do not do what is right, sin is crouching at your door; it *desires* to have you, but you must rule over it" (Gen 4:6-7).

In the context of Cain's contempt toward his brother, *desire* is connected to control, manipulation, force, and takeover. So the curse that Eve must now bear is that she will *desire* her husband; this communicates that she (and all women) will seek to manipulate, control, and at times take over their male partner.[4]

The consequences of the curse are indeed squirm-worthy. Men will rule over women, and women will seek to control men. Sounds like a recipe for decades upon decades of tension between this once-united pair. And we indeed have the recorded history of strife between the two. Devastating, no doubt.

But here's the major idea that is missed. In the *beginning* we see God's perfect ideal for man and woman. After the fall and the associated curses, God never says, "Ah, at last! This is now the ideal. We have finally arrived!" God is not offering up a prescriptive vision for how men and women *ought* to interact. Instead, God is describing the hard reality that will unfold for centuries to come.

In the *beginning* we see God's ideal—man and woman created as equal partners, a cohesive team. But now, because of the fall, there is a power struggle. Men will rule over women by force. And women will seek to manipulate and control. Because of the fall, marriages *will be challenging* as both partners may seek to lord over one another. Throughout the rest of Scripture, we see this glaring reality. We see this in relationships today. #MeToo, #ChurchToo, Harvey Weinstein, Bill Hybels, and the battle of the sexes are just a few examples of this descriptive reality. But never is it God's beautiful *ideal*; rather, it's the backdrop of our everyday reality, and it is the backdrop throughout the story of God. Scot McKnight says,

> The good news story of the Bible is that the broken creation eventually gives way to new creation; the dead can be reborn and re-created; instead of a war of wills there can be a unity of wills. Sadly, the church has far too often perpetuated what is described in Genesis 3:16 as a permanent condition designed by God until the new creation. Perpetuating Genesis 3:16 and the war of the wills with the male ruling

and the female entails failing to restore creation conditions when it comes to male and female relationships. This is against both Jesus and Paul, who each read the Bible as a story that moves from creation (oneness) to new creation (oneness). Reading Genes 3:16 as divine prescription (God's will until the new creation but partly undone with redemption) rather than prediction and description means God has willed women to be the contrarians and men as dominators. This is far from the way of God in the Bible's story: God's redemption means oneness and mutuality, not hierarchy and the war of the wills.[5]

For Christians the reality of the fall should not *dictate* our way of living. We ought not to look to the curses and say, "This is prescriptive for all times, all relationships, all marriages, and all contexts." Instead, as the people of God in Christ, we allow the kingdom vision of Jesus—the gospel—to inform our way of living.

King Jesus stepped into a context where men held all the power and women were viewed as *less than*. A good Jewish man would often pray, "Praise be Thou, O Lord, who did not make me a woman."[6] As Jesus steps in, he establishes alternative paths to the ways of this world. He steps into a broken, sinful, and fractured world and propels us to live toward *God's ideal* and intentions for humankind. Jesus calls us to not use our power to lord it over one another and instead use it to empower, embolden, come alongside, edify, encourage, and extend love, grace, and goodness to one another. Jesus invites us to a *different kind of power* and a different way of living. The power Jesus calls us to is the way of empathy, relinquishment, humility, equality, and reconciliation. Never does Jesus call us to *lord* and *rule* over one another, including between men and women.

Furthermore, Jesus steps into a context where men held *all* the cards, and he audaciously rubs shoulders with women he shouldn't be rubbing shoulders with and emboldens women to share the good news of Jesus. In John 4, Jesus rather intentionally converses with a Samaritan woman in a forsaken place. A Jew—let alone a Jewish teacher—would typically avoid Samaria and would never be caught with a woman. But Jesus sees her for who she is and moves past casual small talk. Instead of judging her or shaming her, he offers her the gift of eternal life. As her secrets come to light, an awakening happens within her. To the very community that was perhaps a source of shame for her, she now returns as one of the first evangelists in the Gospels.

Three days after the cross, one of Jesus' disciples stood outside of the tomb of Jesus and realized he was gone. As she wept, Jesus called out to her,

> "Woman, why are you crying? Who is it you are looking for?"
>
> Thinking he was the gardener, she said, "Sir, if you have carried him away, tell me where you have put him, and I will get him."
>
> Jesus said to her, "Mary."
>
> She turned toward him and cried out in Aramaic, "Rabboni!" (which means "Teacher").
>
> Jesus said, "Do not hold on to me, for I have not yet ascended to the Father. Go instead to my brothers and tell them, 'I am ascending to my Father and your Father, to my God and your God.'"
>
> Mary Magdalene went to the disciples with the news: "I have seen the Lord!" And she told them that he had said these things to her. (Jn 20:15-17)

Imagine the utter exhilaration! I doubt she fully understood that her Easter proclamation would be proclaimed down throughout the centuries, year after year. I doubt she fully understood that she was the first to proclaim the good news of Easter. "He is risen! He's not dead!"

Mary Magdalene, an emboldened evangelist and preacher, was *chosen on purpose* to be the first. We stand in the tradition of Mary. We also stand in the tradition of Deborah, Huldah, Esther, Ruth, Mary, Priscilla, and Junia. This narrative culminates in the person of King Jesus, who makes room for women and men at the table. Time and again, we see the radical nature of Jesus and the Gospel writers elevating the voice and role of women. Rebecca McLaughlin notes,

> The portrayal of women in the Gospels—particularly in Luke's Gospel—is stunningly countercultural. Luke constantly pairs men with women, and when he compares the two, it is almost always in the woman's favor. Before Jesus' birth, two people are visited by the angel Gabriel and told they are going to become parents. One is Zechariah who becomes John the Baptist's father. The other is Jesus' mother Mary. Both ask Gabriel how this can be. But while Zechariah is punished with months of dumbness for his unbelief, Mary is only commended.[7]

Jesus repeatedly affirms the value and worth of women. Jesus empowers and emboldens them to be colaborers in the mission of God. Jesus unabashedly elevated the role of women so they too could participate in the frontline kingdom work. Women of the Bible were indeed emboldened to partner with their brothers.

THIS IS THE GOSPEL

The good news of the gospel is often distorted in our overly individualized culture. As Scot McKnight reminds us, the gospel isn't laid out for one's individual salvation; rather, it's the story of God that culminates in the life, death, resurrection, and ascension of King Jesus and the gift of the Spirit.[8] The implications of the gospel alter who is now included in the once exclusive ethnic Israel. In Christ, the flood gates are opened, the footing is leveled, and an abundant number of chairs are pulled up to the great banquet table. No longer are ethnic Jews alone included in the kingdom, but the ripple effect of the gospel means Jew and Gentile, male and female, slave and free, rich and poor, elite and lowly, and weak and strong are all welcomed to the great banquet table. The vision of the gospel flattens any and all worldly hierarchies and invites us to root ourselves in a subversive, countercultural, and inclusive story. Sadly, our hierarchies that pit men and women against one another diminish the radiant witness of the gospel. We are a *gospel people*, dear brothers and sisters. We gather at the table on equal footing, we sit at the table as brothers and sisters, and we are sent as colaborers.

THIS IS THE MISSION OF GOD

On the day of Pentecost, Peter stood up and declared,

This is what was spoken by the prophet Joel:

"In the last days, God says,
    I will pour out my Spirit on all people.
Your sons and daughters will prophesy,
    your young men will see visions,
    your old men will dream dreams.

Even on my servants, both men and women,
    I will pour out my Spirit in those days,
    and they will prophesy." (Acts 2:14-18)

We people of Pentecost are sent in the fullness of the power of the Spirit to partner with God in the redemption of all of creation. That seems to be a pretty massive job. While it certainly is not up to *us*, God chooses God's people to be the bodies to carry the mission, the mouths to teach and preach the gospel, the hands to heal the sick and set the world aright, and the feet to set captives free. In a weary, broken, and dark world, we are *called*, *sent*, and *commissioned* to participate in this incredible work. When men and women flourish in our Spirit-impelled and -propelled gifts, the church flourishes. When women and men are held back, the church is held back.

In chapter two I shared that sequoia trees need to be rooted in the right environment in order for them to flourish. But there's something else about the sequoias that is essential to their flourishing. A sequoia's root system is complex, massive, and expansive. Their roots extend up to four acres and twenty-feet deep. Not only that, but a sequoia tree *can't* flourish alone. They are found in groves; they are surrounded by hundreds of other giants. As their roots plunge beneath the earth, they are intertwined with other sequoia roots. Together, they are able to withstand storms and winds. Sequoias *need one another* to flourish.

Brothers and sisters, there is a mission at hand, and to flourish, we need *one another*. Our flourishing isn't about *us* but the mission of God and the radiant witness of the gospel. Brothers, partner with your sisters, and sisters, partner with your brothers. This is the radiant gospel; this is the radiant mission. *We get to do this*, not alone but together.

FOCUS ON JESUS

Often, when I talk about women in ministry, someone will inevitably say, "Stop making it about gender, can't we just focus on Jesus?" Sadly, although I've never preached a single sermon on women in ministry in my home pulpit, I still hear this criticism often.

I did not go into ministry to talk about women in ministry. I went into ministry first because of God's call and all the passion that flows out of that call—sharing the good news of the gospel, shepherding the church. I couldn't agree more with the call to focus on Jesus. Amen! Focusing on Jesus has a transformative effect on a person's life, inside and out. When Saul encountered the risen Lord on the road to Damascus, he went from opposing Christ to honoring him. Paul's honoring of Christ transformed his life. Saul was known for breathing murderous threats against anyone who opposed the Torah, and Paul was known for preaching the gospel of Jesus Christ with passion. As he shares in Romans 1:16, "I am not ashamed of the gospel, because it is the power of God that brings salvation to everyone who believes: first to the Jew, then to the Gentile."

For the apostle Paul, focusing on Jesus was indeed *everything.* Paul also knew that focusing on Jesus had massive implications. Paul wrote the entire book of Romans to communicate the implications focusing on Jesus has on the Christ-follower. When we focus on Jesus, we are compelled to make space for those who are not like us or for those with whom we disagree. When we focus on Jesus, we have a vision of what imitating Jesus looks like (Phil 2:5-11). When we focus on Jesus, we discover that worldly hierarchies are flipped on their head and flattened. When we focus on Jesus, we can't help but speak up when we notice parts of the bride of Christ not living the vision of Jesus.

When we focus on Jesus, we are emboldened to live out the kingdom vision as Jesus saw, taught, and believes we can live today. Yes, let's focus on Jesus, and let's faithfully live out, teach, and preach the gospel power.

DEAR RADIANT CHURCH

In closing, I'd like to have a word first with my sisters, second with my brothers, and then with all of us. Gather round, dear sisters, but by all means, listen in, dear brothers.

To my sisters. You are a warrior, my sister.[9]

Oh, you *are* a warrior. You stand on the shoulders of Deborah, Esther, and Mary the mother of Jesus, and Mary Magdalene, Huldah, Jael—the woman with a lion heart—and Junia the bright apostle. These women were by no means weak, but they were "more than conquerors through him who loved us" (Rom 8:37).

These women were wise and listened to their gut instincts. They courageously led the people of Israel and left everything to follow Jesus. They slew giants and boldly spoke on behalf of God's people. They obeyed God when no one else seemingly did. They were brilliant, imaginative, and courageous.

It's possible you are exhausted and discouraged by your attempt to find your place in the church, and you wonder how much longer you can do this. I've been there too. Maybe you've given God ultimatums or screamed and cried so hard in your pillow that you wondered if anyone else heard you.

What if I fail? What if this all falls apart? I can't do this anymore. I'm exhausted. I'm weary. These may be common thoughts you've had.

Dear sister, I pray these words permeate your heart through the gift of the Holy Spirit . . .

You are a warrior in Christ.

You have been given the gift of the Spirit of Pentecost—the very Spirit who shook open the grave where Jesus slept. You have been called by the same God who raised up warriors and leaders like Deborah. If something has stirred in you while reading this chapter, perhaps a larger role within the bride—your heart for proclamation, evangelism, teaching, and leading—isn't merely a childhood fantasy but a holy, chaotic stirring from the Spirit of the living God. It's a stirring that will propel, impel, empower, and embolden you to do things beyond your wildest imagination. So, dear sister, the night won't last. I've seen resurrection in the middle of desolation, and I believe the God who continues to make all things new is *presently calling women to participate in a groundswell we've never seen before*. So rise up, warrior. God has moved. God is moving. And God will continue to move.

One more thing before we end our conversation.

You are also clay.

At the end of the day, you are clay. Consider sweet Hagar (Gen 16; 21), the seemingly forgotten and invisible woman in the narrative of Israel. While the spotlight is on Abram and Sarai, Hagar is mistreated, abused, disenfranchised, and despised. With no rights, no dignity, no freedom, no choice, she's finally had enough and runs. As she's at the well weeping, an angel of the Lord sees her and speaks tenderly to her, and she cries out vulnerably, "You are the God who sees me. . . . I have now seen the One who sees me" (Gen 16:13).

Dear warrior, you are also clay. Perhaps you find yourself running, vulnerable, or exhausted. The God who sees is a mere whisper away. In your frailty, vulnerability, and weakness, you *will fail* if you do this *without* the God who sees.

You have *nothing* to prove, and you have nothing to give other than the power of the Spirit. The courage, strength, and power you are looking for is a prayer away, and whatever you do, do pray. Remember why you have decided to do this to begin with. Remember our first love, and fall in love with Jesus more and more as each day passes. Return to the Scriptures, fall on your knees, dance with your Savior, and delight in his presence.

God *does* see you, and God sees *you without the titles, the degrees, and the platform*. God sees into the depths of your heart and dreams, and God loves every bit of it.

Dear sister, you are clay. Tune your heart to God's heart in the morning when you rise and in your moments, breaths, and steps— for without Jesus, all of this is meaningless. Perhaps you need to be reminded that you need him more than acceptance and titles. Return to *his love, and bask in the presence of the God who sees you and delights in you.*

Dear sister, you are a warrior, and you are also clay. Go now and live into this gospel reality that God has stirred in your soul, and do it as a warrior but also as clay.

To my brothers. Dear brothers, I hope you listened in on my word to my sisters. I can understand how sometimes when we talk about emboldening women in ministry, it would seem like we are trying to force our way without you. I understand that it might feel like we are trying to take over, but that couldn't be further from the truth. In order for us to live out this gospel reality, we desperately need you, your partnership, your gifts, and your voice. You also need us, our partnership, our gifts, and our voice. This isn't women versus men; neither is it a battle. This is about all of us bearing witness to the gospel of King Jesus and living on mission in ways that enable flourishing. So you might be wondering what you can do. Here are a few things to consider:

If you are in leadership, surround yourself with both gifted women and men.

If you are not in leadership, talk to your pastor about empowering women by seating them at the table where your pastor sits.

Come to terms with and admit any biases you might have toward women.

Find ways to encourage women in your congregation who have potential gifts of teaching, leading, and preaching.

Read and learn from your sisters.

To the church. This battle—which is not of flesh and blood—summons brothers to join their sisters and sisters to join their brothers so they can be warriors in Christ. Sisters, along with their brothers, are emboldened by the Spirit of Pentecost to be on the frontlines of mission. The radiant gospel has beautiful implications for the people of God, and we are merely living out a distorted vision when we exclude gifted sisters from the table.

People of God, let us bear witness to the most radiant and beautiful gospel.

QUESTIONS FOR INDIVIDUALS AND GROUPS

1. Why is the author passionate about women in ministry?

2. What is God's ideal for man and woman?

3. If the fall is the *backdrop* of the story of God, how does this change the way we view the relationship between men and women in this world?

4. What is the full meaning of *ezer?*

5. If a woman is *ezer,* does this mean subordinance?

6. How has the reality of the fall impacted relationships between men and women?

7. What can our brothers do to come alongside their sisters for the sake of the mission?

7

RADIANT EVANGELISM

IN THE LATE 1990s I met Jesus while reading the Gospel of Luke. Meeting Jesus flipped my world upside down and turned it inside out. Naturally, I wanted *everyone* around me to experience what I experienced, to see what I had seen, and to know who I had come to know. I was a teenager when the song "Jesus Freak" first came out, and I was so proud to be a Jesus freak that my best girlfriends and I made T-shirts that said "Jesus Freak #1," "Jesus Freak #2," and "Jesus Freak #3." I not only loved the song by DC Talk, but I also read the book *Jesus Freaks*, which told the stories of Christians who were martyred for their faith. It gripped me because I wanted nothing more than to be the kind of Christian that would take a stand as the martyrs did.

My friends and I were so on fire for our faith that we began a prayer movement at our school. We rallied around our school flagpole at nine o'clock every night for prayer. One night as we were praying, a car drove by and threw a cup full of soda and ice at us. I was happy—we were being "persecuted" for our faith.

I continued to become emboldened to share my faith. My youth leaders from Youth for Christ took me through evangelism classes so I could know how to clearly articulate the gospel to my friends and family. I learned the "Romans Road," the "Sinner's Prayer," the "Bridge diagram," and how to clearly articulate my testimony. When it came to evangelism in my teen years, I was a force to be reckoned with. I was prepared at any given moment to convince someone of their need for Jesus. It wasn't uncommon for my friends and me to invade the local Kmart and do evangelism street style.

Many nights I would come home from school, plop open my Bible at the dinner table, and tell my parents that unless they were born again, I would not be able to spend an eternity with them in heaven. Thumping them over the head with the Bible seemed to be my best tactic. To me, Jesus was Lord, end of story, no argument. If I could quote a few compelling Bible verses, convince someone of their sinfulness, and help them see their need for Jesus, then just maybe they would convert. I wasn't ashamed of good scare tactics or forceful communication methods.

As the Spirit often does, it worked through my forceful evangelism methods, but only by God's grace. Somehow, I believed I knew exactly what everyone needed, and I did little listening. The Bible was a weapon I passionately used to beat others over the head.

I repent.

This style of evangelism is one that many young people are repulsed by today. Bring up evangelism to a group of millennials and many will likely shake their heads in disgust. Some of the many problems include coercive shortcuts and treating others as a project.

Recently, a Barna study revealed that

> Almost half of Millennials (47%) agree at least somewhat that it is wrong to share one's personal beliefs with someone of a different faith in hopes that they will one day share the same faith. This is compared to a little over one-quarter of Gen X (27%), and one in five Boomers (19%) and Elders (20%).[1]

In the church, there are many who lament the way evangelism has been lost. When I first read this study, I was troubled. We are Great Commission people, though it seems that many would rather embrace the Great Commandment but avoid the Great Commission. To be clear, however, what many young people are reacting to is *a hurtful form of evangelism.*

Many believe that evangelism is rooted in a forceful form of colonialism. To put it simply, colonialism suggests there are right and wrong or good and bad cultures. Often, when European settlers colonized the new world, they believed that the native peoples needed to not only become Christians but become *like them.* Conquest, assimilation, and lording over other cultures is a sad history we must not forget. Noemi Vega Quiñones, coauthor of *Hermanas,* writes:

> While we have learned helpful ways of sharing our faith, some of our hearers may still be pained and even turned away from the gospel by the way Christianity has been pained in the past. The history of colonization is one to remember and learn from, lest we repeat the same mistakes. We must acknowledge and remember where evangelistic efforts begin to go wrong. Our Christian witness falls short when we abandon love as the center of our Great Commission.[2]

Furthermore, in many forms of evangelism, the evangelist is in a posture of dominance through their speeches, arguments, propositions, and rhetoric. But we *are* Great Commission people. We *have* been commissioned to make disciples, and we are sent out to the ends of the earth to be Christ's witnesses (Acts 1:8). I am profoundly concerned over the present reluctance to evangelize, just as I am profoundly concerned about our past practices that have caused harm and our disposition toward shortcuts and easy tactics. The news we have been commissioned to share is, after all, the best news. James Choung says,

> Good news is not meant to be held back. We're wired to tell someone about it. Whether it's a good book, an inspiring movie, a job promotion, a luxurious getaway, a catchy song, an exhilarating hike or a random encounter with an old friend, we really can't wait to grab someone and load them up with the details.[3]

RECLAIMING ANGUISH FOR THE LOST

In Romans 9–10 the apostle Paul is in utter anguish over his Jewish brothers and sisters because of their blatant rejection of the gospel of King Jesus. For Paul, King Jesus is the culmination of the story of Israel, and yet the people of Israel refuse to receive the gift offered in Christ. In these chapters, Paul expresses his intense desire to see his people receive Jesus as their Messiah. He experiences so much grief that he would even be willing to be "cut off" so that his people can be saved. He writes,

> I speak the truth in Christ—I am not lying, my conscience confirms it through the Holy Spirit—I have great sorrow and unceasing anguish in my heart. For I could wish that I

myself were cursed and cut off from Christ for the sake of my people, those of my own race, the people of Israel. Theirs is the adoption to sonship; theirs the divine glory, the covenants, the receiving of the law, the temple worship and the promises. Theirs are the patriarchs, and from them is traced the human ancestry of the Messiah, who is God over all, forever praised! Amen. (Rom 9:1-5)

So many Christians have lost a deep sense of anguish for those who have yet to receive the good news of King Jesus. This could be due to busy schedules, fear of rejection, or concern about causing more harm than good. But the proclamation of the gospel was central to Paul's ministry, and he grieved for those who did not receive Jesus. Paul understood that Jesus is God's life-giving and community-restoring gift, and anyone who calls on the name of the Lord will indeed be saved (Rom 10:13). We—the church—have a role in sharing this good news. As Paul says, "How, then, can they believe in the one of whom they have not heard? And how can they hear without someone preaching to them? And how can anyone preach unless they are sent? As it is written: 'How beautiful are the feet of those who bring good news!'" (Rom 10:14-15).

I believe we have knowledge of the best news in the world. God's people are sent people—sent to bring, proclaim, and bear the good news. There is good news to share for a dark, desperate, despair-ridden, weary world. C. S. Lewis beautifully says,

The Church exists for nothing else but to draw [people] into Christ, to make them little Christs. If they are not doing that, all the cathedrals, clergy, missions, sermons, even the Bible itself, are simply a waste of time. God became Man for no other purpose. It is even doubtful, you know, whether the whole universe was created for any other purpose. It says in the Bible that the whole universe was made for Christ and that everything is to be gathered together in Him.[4]

We have a role to play, but it's tempting to think otherwise. We must remember that we are both a gathered people and a sent people. We are sent—called to participate in the redemption of all of creation. If our news is good news, and if our tactics have been harmful, what do we do? How do we share the news of the gospel?

RECLAIMING THE GIFT OF RELATIONSHIPS

Let's begin with relationships. Perhaps most importantly, relationships aren't about a means to an end—that is, a task or a project. Relationships with our neighbors should never be an agenda to accomplish; rather, the value of relationships is because community is a gift, friendships are a gift, and neighborliness is a gift. True friendships see past differences in beliefs, ideology, and lifestyle choices. Relational evangelism, although well-meaning, has become agenda- and project-driven, and our neighbors have not been fooled. Evangelism must always be born out of love.

My friend Kim is one of those people who makes everyone feel like they are the most important person in the room. She also loves her church and probably wants to see it grow more than anyone. But her friendships in her work environment, neighborhood, and school is not about getting butts in the pews. Neither is it about building friendships for conversion. Kim loves people, and people know that when they are around her. Kim shows her love by helping other mamas with school pickup or volunteering to help set up a party or throwing a neighborhood pool party or going out of her way to help a distressed coworker. Kim is also an evangelist. There have been several occasions when she has shared her love for King Jesus with a neighbor, but it's never because she sees the neighbor as a project or means to an end. Evangelism, for Kim, comes out of sincere love and neighborliness.

But before she shares the good news of Jesus, she embodies the gospel power in all that she does. Before words, she bears witness to the love, joy, peace, patience, kindness, goodness, gentleness, and generosity of the kingdom. When reduced to a presentation, the gospel is severely malnourished. The gospel is something we bear witness to, something we embody, and something we live. By the time Kim shares the good news verbally, it has been seen.

When we show up in our neighbors' lives, when we listen to them, when we love them, trust is earned, and it becomes clear that we are there to build relationships, not agendas. We are there to love, not convert. No one wants to feel like a project, a prize to be won, or item on an agenda to be checked off when completed. As long as we see our neighbors that way, we will treat them that way. Instead, entering into their worlds incarnationally, we listen deeply enough to see life through their eyes. Eventually, if we do have the impulse to share the good news of Jesus, it is birthed out of love instead of any ulterior motives. Evangelism must always be rooted in authentic love.

LIVING INCARNATIONALLY

We often rely on shortcuts for a quick result. Why? Because shallow tactics don't require us to enter into the lives of our neighbors. It's easy to ask a neighbor to come into *my world* than it is to enter into *theirs*. That is, it's much easier to pass out a flier and invite a neighbor to a church event than it is to show up in their lives and be in relationship for the long haul. Often, we ask our neighbors to come to our church event or come to our worship service, but we rarely show care or concern for their needs, desires, and cares.

What if we instead enter into the world of the culture around us? Anyone who has studied missiology knows that an understanding of the culture around us is critical. We have to understand the language around us, and to do that, it requires rubbing shoulders with the world around us.

We live in a pluralistic world, and this world cannot be forced into believing truth that it may not have language for. Instead, we must learn others' language and culture. Lesslie Newbigin compares the process of learning the language of others to that of a child learning to speak:

> A missionary or anthropologist who really hopes to understand and enter into the adopted culture will not do so by trying to learn the language in a way tourist uses a phrase book and a dictionary. It must be learned in the way a child learns to speak, not by finding words to match one's existing stock, but by learning to think and speak in the way the people of the country do.[5]

Our call is to be incarnate in the world around us—living in the presence and the power of the Spirit while listening and seeking to understand our neighbors. Michael Frost explains:

> The term mission (from the Latin word *missio*) means "to be sent; to be propelled outward." Lots of churches seem to get

the idea that to be *missional* we must mean to go out to others with the Good News, rather than merely wait for people to come to us. But the term *incarnational* refers to another dimension of mission. It describes not simply going out but also the difficult work of going deep with others. Just as God took on flesh and dwelt among us in Jesus, so his followers are called to *dwell among* those whom they're sent.[6]

Jesus "moved into the neighborhood" and dwelt among his neighbors (Jn 1:14 *The Message*). To live incarnationally is to tend to our neighbors as we tend to the presence of Jesus. It propels us outward to move into the world around us—to see them, know them, listen to them, seek to understand them, and love them.[7]

These days it seems Christians make snap judgments about the culture around us. For example, I often hear things like "Millennials these days . . ." but I'm not always certain that those saying this truly understand millennials. This certainly can be said the other way around for any generation making snap judgments about another generation. It's not just generations but also religions, lifestyle choices, gender dynamics, and political choices.

All of this requires the Christian to actually have relationships outside of the church. While this might seem like a no-brainer, it's clear that so many struggle with this. Many Christians don't have a single non-Christian friend. It's easier and safer to remain in the safe bubble of our Christian world—that is, go to church, talk to our Christian friends, break bread with Christian friends, call on Christian plumbers and realtors, support Christian businesses, go to Christian schools, participate in Christian organizations, and listen to Christian music. Eventually, it's easy to lose touch with culture and become completely unrelatable to the world around us. We then assume we know everything we need to know about our neighbors. We do little to no studying of our culture and the world around us. This then leads to a lack of understanding of the world our neighbors live in, and eventually we are more known for what we are against than what we are for.

What if Christians reclaim anguish for our lost neighbors and also curiosity about their cultures. That is, curiosity that leads to loving, to knowing, and to understanding. If we want to see the world turn their lives over to King Jesus, it actually requires us to rub shoulders with those who are not in the church. It requires us to hear their stories, cry with them, walk with them, and care for them.

Presence is one of the greatest gifts we can give anyone. Let's show up in people's lives—their homes, celebrations, important events, and through the gift of listening. When we do this and listen, we begin to understand their needs, their longings, and their hopes.

SHARING THE RADIANT GOSPEL

Sharing the gospel has often been thought of as a formulaic, step-by-step presentation. First, convince someone of their terrible sinfulness. Second, help them see how there is no possible way for them to dig themselves out of their terrible sinful hole. Third, tell them they are destined for hell. Fourth, tell them that the only way out is to accept Jesus Christ as their Lord and Savior. Fifth, guide them through the sinner's prayer.

Certainly, this style of evangelism has been efficacious for a particular era among a particular culture. In fact, the very first time I ever heard the Four Spiritual Laws was couched within the Bridge diagram. The Youth for Christ director told me there was no way I could ever climb my way out of the sinful hole I was in. It was only by way of the cross and opening my heart to Jesus that I would have any chance of entering through the pearly gates of heaven. The Spirit planted some seeds in my heart that day which eventually led to a life of living for Jesus. But if I had tried that kind of gospel presentation on my neighbors in Southern California, it would have been like trying to fit a square peg in a round hole. It would have been an inauthentic shortcut that would have led to, at best, a shallow response and, at worst, blatant rejection.

Sharing the good news involves bearing witness to a story that has significant ramifications. Scot McKnight tells us that sharing the gospel is to "herald, to proclaim, and to declare something about something.... [T]he gospel is to announce good news about key events in the life of Jesus Christ. The gospel for Paul was to tell, announce, declare, and shout aloud the story of Jesus Christ as the saving news of God."[8]

Sharing the good news of the gospel—evangelism—means to announce what God has done in Christ. Of course, this is born out of love, relationship, and then promptings and leadings from the Holy Spirit. When we announce the good news to those we love, to those we know, and to those we are in relationship with, and when we do this empowered by the Spirit, we aren't merely sharing in a top-down manner but in a way that generates meaningful conversation. Often, when we share the gospel, we are sharing something we know, we have seen, and we have experienced. We have seen the power the gospel has to heal, reconcile, and redeem. Sharing the gospel must be born out of experience and behavior.

The apostle Peter says,

> In your hearts revere Christ as Lord. Always be prepared to give an answer to everyone who asks you to give the reason for the hope that you have. But do this with gentleness and

respect, keeping a clear conscience, so that those who speak maliciously against your good behavior in Christ may be ashamed of their slander. (1 Pet 3:15-16)

In Southern California Christians occasionally experience hostility. Some of my friends have valid concerns about what they see of and hear about Christians. Hypocrisy, moral superiority, and boundary markers are some of the things that repulse my friends outside of the church. I have one friend, Jenny, who was wary of me when she found out I am a pastor. She put up a wall almost immediately, and it took a while for her to warm up to me.

Eventually, though, she and I bonded over a shared crisis with our children's teacher at our neighborhood school. We had coffee several times and bemoaned the situation but also celebrated the blossoming friendship between our boys. It seemed that over time Jenny forgot I was a pastor and saw me as another mama from the school. She eventually opened up to me about her bitterness toward the church. She has been hurt by so-called Christians and is repulsed by Christians who align themselves with politicians, power, and partisan causes. I think her hostility was understandable and tragic. In Jenny's adult life she had never seen a life that bore witness to the gracious, loving King. She had encountered Christians who attempted to share their faith, and these experiences only left her feeling bitter.

Evangelism isn't an intellectual or cognitive proposition detached from one's lifestyle. It's sharing the gospel born out of a *gospel life*—that is, a life transformed and continually shaped by the gospel. Evangelism happens when we are *caught up* in something bigger than ourselves.[9]

It isn't that we aren't to use words. Words are important and generating conversations about Jesus is very important. Use words. Are we to testify that Jesus is the way? For sure. Do we tell the story of Jesus, his life, the story of Israel, the cross, the resurrection, and the gift of the Spirit? Definitely. Do we proclaim that Jesus is alive? Yes. When sharing the gospel, we ought to use words. Preach the gospel, but let the preaching be born out of our life and deeds. May we "become the gospel" so we will have "opportunities to speak the gospel."[10]

During one conversation over coffee with Jenny, she asked what I was up to that day. I told her about a project we had been working on at church to partner with an organization that welcomes unaccompanied children crossing the US-Mexico border. We had been working on the partnership for several months and was preparing to open its doors for a daytime daycare with wraparound services and then foster care with church families.

As I shared with her about the work we were doing, Jenny's eyes welled up. She said, "Are you kidding me? You're making me cry. I never knew that Christians even cared about immigration. I never knew Christians cared about these children, and now you're telling me your church is doing something about it!"

That opened the door for me to tell her that I believed it was a *mandate* for the church to care for those children. I told her about the Jesus I fell in love with, and Jesus was calling us to do this. As the conversation went on, she openly expressed how shocking this was. The Christians she knew were not so compassionate and appeared to be more against causes and people than they were *for people*. The conversation then got sweeter.

I then shared the gospel with Jenny—that is, the good news of Jesus in his life, death, resurrection, and ascension. Because of this incredible news, I said, God's table is long and includes the stranger and immigrant. In the Gospels, Jesus was *for* the "least of these." I then said that someday those who die with Christ will also be raised to new life, and we will join Christ in the new heaven and new earth, where there will be *no more sorrow*, no more refugees, no more child immigrants, no more pain, and no more broken families. And while Christians look forward to that day, we don't wait; rather, we partner with Jesus *now* as he builds a kingdom that looks more like the future.

Tears fell from Jenny's face and onto the coffee table. There was a shift in her spirit and a softening of her heart that day. While my old Youth for Christ counterparts might have thought that wasn't a gospel presentation, I beg to differ. I shared the good news of the gospel that day, and I believe Jenny may have seen a glimpse of Jesus in my testimony. She also heard it in the actions of the church.

CONTEXTUALIZING THE GOSPEL

The implications of the gospel are life-altering, game-changing, and earth-shattering. The implications of the good news are so much more than getting into heaven. It entails participating in embodying heaven on earth. It is partnering with God to restore shalom in the Godforsaken spaces in this world, opening a home for a weary child after crossing the border, opening a space at the table to a reluctant seeker, and feeding the hungry who are stuck in systemic poverty.

In Southern California, contextualizing the gospel looks a lot like my story with Jenny. While there was a time when gospel presentations required helping people see their own sin and repent, today, people don't necessarily *feel* sinful, and most won't be shamed into confession. The gospel is good news for *everyone*, no matter where they are in life or what they are going through. So we must ask ourselves, *What are they going through right now?* Some may need to hear about Jesus the restorer of broken hearts, and some might need to hear about the radical inclusion of the gospel, and some might need to hear about Jesus offering rest for the weary, while others desperately need to know that someday Jesus will make the world just and right again. Cookie-cutter evangelism methods are void of discernment and contextualization.

More than ever Christians must practice kingdom living in their own neighborhoods and always be ready to "give an answer to everyone who asks you to give the reason for the hope that you have." The gospel story is robust and reaches every human on earth. Therefore, we must be ready to share this story with the language of those we speak with so they can relate to, understand, and celebrate the gospel. It's good news! How will we tell the good news story to our neighbors?

This is the story we get to tell, and this is how we get to use our words in evangelism. When I share the gospel with my friends, these are the stories I tell. Heaven is bursting forth on earth through the church, and the powers of darkness are being dismantled. This is my story. This is my song.

PRAY FOR THE MINISTRY OF EVANGELISM

The apostle Paul both grieved for the lost and also urgently desired to share the good news. He believed that we ought to pray for our neighbors and for opportunities to share the gospel. In Colossians 4:2-6, Paul writes,

> Devote yourselves to prayer, being watchful and thankful. And pray for us, too, that God may open a door for our message, so that we may proclaim the mystery of Christ, for which I am in chains. Pray that I may proclaim it clearly, as

I should. Be wise in the way you act toward outsiders; make the most of every opportunity. Let your conversation be always full of grace, seasoned with salt, so that you may know how to answer everyone. (Col 4:2-6)

Every week I see a lot of prayer-request lists, and while everything on those lists matter, I grieve that rarely are there requests to pray for the proclamation of the gospel to our neighbors. The North American church is facing an evangelism crisis, and there is no greater place to counter this than on our knees. When we pray for the evangelistic ministry of the church, our own hearts, minds, and eyes are changed. As the Spirit shapes our hearts, they begin to ache and yearn for the things God's heart aches and yearns for, and we begin to see our neighbors as God sees them. And we become more aware of open doors to share the message.

A while back a dear friend and I began going on prayer walks around our kids' schools. We circled the school block and prayed for not only our kids but for potential evangelistic ministry. It wasn't that we suddenly saw families giving their lives to Jesus, but it changed our own hearts and perspectives. We were more sensitive to opportunities to connect with families and more sensitive to the Spirit's leading in all conversations.

Many evenings my family and I walk through our neighborhood. While we walk I pray for our neighbors as we pass their homes. I not only pray that they would come to know Jesus, but I pray for open doors and opportunities. Praying for my neighbors helps me carefully and lovingly tend to the needs of my neighbors as I listen to the prompting of the Spirit. When I lived in Southern California, I was grateful for the friendships we made in our neighborhood, and I was in awe of the ways the Spirit moved. Several neighbors became involved in life at PazNaz and discovered what it meant to walk with Jesus. We must *pray for the ministry of evangelism in our churches, in our neighborhoods, and in our workplaces.*

Dear church, it's time we reclaim the evangelistic ministry of the church for a new day. We are *sent ones*, and we are Great Commission people. We are called and commissioned to partner with God in proclaiming life-altering and game-changing news. We are not called to sit back and do nothing. Neither are we called to be lords, to coerce others, or to make declarations. Gospel proclamation is a sacred, Spirit-filled, and Spirit-led act, born out of love and relationship.

QUESTIONS FOR INDIVIDUALS AND GROUPS

1. When you think of evangelism, what comes to mind?

2. In what ways has the idea of evangelism been used in coercive ways?

3. Have you ever experienced "shallow tactics" for evangelism? What was the result?

4. What would it look like for evangelism to be reclaimed for a new day?

5. What might it look like to have an anguish for the lost today?

6. Imagine a new kind of evangelism explosion in your community. What would it look like? How would it be different from evangelism twenty or thirty years ago?

8

RADIANT PRACTICES

IN THE SUMMER OF 2009, I became passionate about training for and competing in triathlons (swimming, biking, running). I was a swimmer for my entire life, so I figured that since I had one of the hardest disciplines down, triathlons would be easy for me.

I read all of the books, I joined a club, and I nerded out on all things triathlon. The first race I signed up for was the Chicago Triathlon, which includes a swim in Lake Michigan, a bike ride on Lake Shore Drive, and a run through the winding sidewalks of the South Loop. To prepare, I changed my diet, my sleeping habits, and my schedule. I woke up early to go for long runs and tempo runs, and I ended my day with forty-plus mile bike rides. I swam over a mile at least three times a week, and I did core training.

As the race was looming, I met for lunch with my friend Katie, who was a seasoned triathlete. I proudly shared with her how I had stayed on schedule with my training plan, and I was confident that I would be ready for the race.

Katie looked at me reluctantly and said, "But I think you're missing one really important step in your training."

"How?" I asked. "I've done *everything by the book.*" I began reciting to her every step I had taken when she interrupted me, "But have you trained in Lake Michigan yet?"

I responded somewhat defensively, "Well, no, but I'm a seasoned swimmer. I was conference champ in the five hundred-yard freestyle!" Katie gently explained to me that a swimming pool was nothing like the turbulent waters of Lake Michigan.

Turned out, she was right. The Chicago Triathlon is at the end of August, so at the end of July I made my way to Chicago to practice in the lake. My body was shocked by both the cold temperatures, the choppy waters, and the occasional swells. While I had trained and trained and trained, I was not prepared in the least bit for waves collapsing on top of me or swells carrying me up and then abruptly down, and I wasn't familiar with swimming in water where I couldn't see. I zigzagged every which way. I swam away from the shore toward the shore. I swam like a pinball in a pinball machine.

That day I learned that even the most experienced swimmers struggle in open-water swimming. I didn't know that there was something called "sighting," where swimmers must be able to lift their eyes to see where they are going. I learned that I needed to pick a target, and every few strokes I needed to pull my head and upper body above water to look for that target and swim toward it.

Choppier water proves to be even more challenging because the swimmer is at risk of taking in a mouthful of water. Not only that but being in big open water can prove to be scary and tear down the confidence of an experienced swimmer. So with just a month left, I trained as much as I could for the open-water swim.

When the day of the race came, it was clear *many* swimmers had not prepared well for the open-water swim. Sadly, many were pulled out of the water by lifeguards in canoes. It's one thing to train for a triathlon in a pool, but it doesn't prepare a swimmer for the changing and shifting tide in open water.

All musicians and athletes know the critical nature of practice. Christians too must *practice* our faith. However, I have concerns that we aren't practicing our faith for the shifting demographics—the choppy waters, the turbulent journey, and the shifting sand. *Our context is turbulent*, but our practices often don't reflect formation and preparation for a changing context. It's no wonder, then, we are seemingly drowning or in over our heads.

There's a storm at sea, and many simply don't know what to do. This storm is fierce, it's chaotic, it's causing damage, and it's yet another reminder of our broken and fallen world. The disciples were not strangers to storms.

In Matthew 8, the disciples are in a storm-tossed boat, but Jesus calms the storm. In Matthew 14:22-33, the disciples find themselves in yet another storm, and Jesus is at first nowhere in sight.

> Jesus made the disciples get into the boat and go on ahead of him to the other side, while he dismissed the crowd. After he had dismissed them, he went up on a mountainside by himself to pray. Later that night, he was there alone, and the boat was already a considerable distance from land, buffeted by the waves because the wind was against it.
>
> Shortly before dawn Jesus went out to them, walking on the lake. When the disciples saw him walking on the lake, they were terrified. "It's a ghost," they said, and cried out in fear.
>
> But Jesus immediately said to them: "Take courage! It is I. Don't be afraid."

"Lord, if it's you," Peter replied, "tell me to come to you on the water."

"Come," he said.

Then Peter got down out of the boat, walked on the water and came toward Jesus. But when he saw the wind, he was afraid and, beginning to sink, cried out, "Lord, save me!"

Immediately Jesus reached out his hand and caught him. "You of little faith," he said, "why did you doubt?"

And when they climbed into the boat, the wind died down. Then those who were in the boat worshiped him, saying, "Truly you are the Son of God."

The disciples feared the sea as a terrifying place—a black abyss of death that threatened the beauty, glory, and goodness of life. The sea was chaotic, evil, and terrifying and represented everything that opposed God. In Matthew 14:24, we see that the wind and the waves are against the disciples. And then, in the darkest hour of the night, a ghostlike figure makes his way toward the disciples. Terrifying, no doubt.

But the figure turns out to be Jesus, and as he comes toward the boat he reveals himself as the one who overcomes the powers of darkness, evil, and chaos. In the midst of the disciples' fear, Jesus declares, "It is I." A voice of assurance in the middle of the chaos.

And then Jesus summons Peter from the boat to face the storm. Peter courageously takes a leap of faith *into* the chaos, but there was no way he could be ready for such a feat. The moment the waves get in his head and he turns his eyes from Jesus and to the chaos, the waves envelop him. Peter sinks and cries out; Jesus rescues him.

This, perhaps, was the most challenging and terrifying moment Peter had experienced in following Jesus. It's not that there weren't challenges, but he wasn't prepared to walk on chaotic waters.

New Testament scholar M. Eugene Boring notes that the entire narrative reflects the conflict between the kingdom of God and the kingdom of Satan. The chaos of the waters hitting the boat represents conflict for the church of the future.[1] Was Jesus preparing Peter and the disciples for the conflict, chaos, and persecution that the early church would eventually experience? Jesus *did say* they would have trouble in this world (Jn 16:33). And certainly, the history of the early church tells us that they *did* face chaos and trouble. Like any good teacher, Jesus was preparing the disciples to practice rising above turbulent waters.

Today, there are chaotic waters crashing against the church, and sadly it seems that the waters are shaking the church to its core. Here's a bit of good news for us: the wind and the waves never once capsized the boat, and the wind and the waves didn't *consume* Peter. So it is for us today! The rains will come, the floodwaters will rise, the storm will beat at the door, the winds will keep howling, the waves will be choppy, and the chaos could get worse. When Peter confessed Jesus as the Messiah, Jesus promised, "I tell you that you are Peter, and on this rock I will build my church, and the gates of Hades will not overcome it" (Mt 16:18). This is a promise we can rely on.

Knowing that the chaos won't die down anytime soon, perhaps we need to consider practices that sustain the church through the chaos. Practices that equip and empower us to rise above the darkness with our eyes on Jesus.

EXAMINE THE STORM IN OUR HEARTS

Perhaps one of the more troubling things I have observed as a pastor is that the church has contributed toward and participated in much of the tumult. We have participated and often have led in racist movements, oppression, and brutality. It's time we start *naming* it. Pastor Faith Romasco, a gifted pastor, often says, "Name it to tame it." There is indeed a storm howling, and the storm is racism. This is something we—the White church—have been avoiding for far too long, and it's time to name it, confess, lament, and repent.

At times this is even more troubling for me as a pastor: we don't know and we don't see the ways we have contributed toward the chaos. Whether by denial or through implicit or complicit thoughts or actions, we are swimming so deep in toxic waters that we can't see straight any longer. As the people of God, we must be willing to bravely and boldly take a fresh look at the situation and see the storm howling. This storm is a principality and power that lurks in systems and structures that far too many of us cannot see.

One of the problems behind racism is most people do not believe they are racist. "Don't call *me* a racist," someone will inevitably say, "my college roommate was a person of color!" Then a case is made as to why someone isn't a racist and how racism is only history. Sean Palmer says this about our denial:

> At root, I believe, is that to our white Christian sisters and brothers naming racism is something like Beetlejuice: if they say it three times out loud it'll appear and demand to be dealt with. Sorrowfully, the failure to name racism doesn't keep us from dealing with bigotry. It actually gives bigotry a stronger hold on us.[2]

Dealing with racism is uncomfortable, and whenever I bring it up, someone will accuse me of being divisive or even racist just by naming it. But we must keep talking about it, we must keep naming it, we can't keep sweeping it under the rug, and we must lament the dark grip it has in our world. The sin and evil of racism isn't only a thing of the past, but it infects our own individual hearts and minds, and it has gripped structural systems throughout our world. When we take a look, we must be willing to admit the ways we have contributed to the storm.

I am often struck by the story of Zacchaeus in Luke 19:

> Jesus entered Jericho and was passing through. A man was there by the name of Zacchaeus; he was a chief tax collector and was wealthy. He wanted to see who Jesus was, but because he was short he could not see over the crowd. So he ran ahead and climbed a sycamore-fig tree to see him, since Jesus was coming that way.
>
> When Jesus reached the spot, he looked up and said to him, "Zacchaeus, come down immediately. I must stay at your house today." So he came down at once and welcomed him gladly.
>
> All the people saw this and began to mutter, "He has gone to be the guest of a sinner."
>
> But Zacchaeus stood up and said to the Lord, "Look, Lord! Here and now I give half of my possessions to the poor, and if I have cheated anybody out of anything, I will pay back four times the amount."
>
> Jesus said to him, "Today salvation has come to this house, because this man, too, is a son of Abraham. For the Son of Man came to seek and to save the lost." (Lk 19:1-10)

Zacchaeus, to many, was a deviant sinner. He was a tax collector of tax collectors, and it would have been assumed that he was dishonest. He would have employed others to collect taxes in the hope of making a profit for the chief tax collector. Zacchaeus was complicit in a system of oppression. What's stunning, however, is when Zacchaeus stands before Jesus, he immediately examines his own life, confesses, and repents. He very quickly understands that he has participated in an evil structure. He also moves forward to *make things right*. "Look, Lord! Here and now I give half of my possessions to the poor, and if I have cheated anybody out of anything, I will pay back four times the amount."

This is hard for us to admit, but in many corners of the church we have participated in systems of oppression, division, polarization, and racism. Like any broken relationship, refusing to take responsibility—in the long term—causes more harm and over time makes matter worse. Sadly, sometimes offenders in broken relationships not only refuse to take responsibility but also minimize a situation or point the finger in another direction.

It's time the White church, in particular, takes on the practice of examen in a fresh way. Examen has been a practice of the church for centuries. It is the process of opening oneself to the Lord so the Spirit might search our hearts, as the psalmist says in Psalm 139:23-24:

> Search me, God, and know my heart;
>   test me and know my anxious thoughts.
> See if there is any offensive way in me,
>   and lead me in the way everlasting.

When we open ourselves up before the living God, the Spirit works to uncover areas in our hearts and minds that may need cleansing, healing, or reworking. Richard Foster notes that deep introspection without God has its problems: "If we are the lone examiners of our heart, a thousand justifications will arise to declare our innocence.... If left to our own devices, it is easy for us to take one good look at who we truly are and declare ourselves unredeemable."[3]

Growing up, when I learned about and used the practice of examen, I usually focused on my own personal sins. I focused on whether or not *I* had lied, whether *I* had lustful thoughts, whether *I* cheated, or whether *I* coveted someone else's possessions. No doubt, this is an important practice that we must all do. However, I never wondered whether *I* benefited or contributed to a system that harmed others. Sometimes we need to zoom the lens out just a bit.

Sadly, although we may *like* people of color, this argument fails to recognize the ways we participate in *systems* that marginalize entire cultures, people groups, and people of color. The White church, for example, stands on a toxic history of segregation, marginalization, and oppression of entire people groups. Throughout history the White church has justified slavery, celebrated lynchings, opposed the civil rights movement, and turned a blind eye to the mass incarceration of Black and Brown bodies.[4] Soong-Chan Rah holds up a mirror for the church to see itself with clarity:

> When white evangelicals abandoned the city in the twentieth century and fled to the suburbs, many assumed that the presence of God had also fled the city. The modern city was seen as devoid of God's presence. There was an assumption that new Jerusalems were being established in the suburbs with the concomitant buildings and new and

impressive houses of worship. In time, the narrative of a city without hope became a part of the modern-day vernacular. Modern-day evangelicals look upon the city with an assumption that the city is spiritually dead.... [T]wentieth century evangelicals began to weave a narrative of distrust and suspicion of the city. The abandonment of the city by twentieth-century evangelicals distanced them from the stories of the "have-nots" and other suffering communities. Instead of finding YHWH still indwelling the city, American evangelicals engaged in a bodily passivity and disconnect in the safe confines of suburban life.[5]

We—the White church—have failed to recognize our participation in evil, oppressive, and racist systems. Racism has taken root in the heart of White evangelicalism while the Spirit continues to speak, "Sin is crouching at your door." We can continue to deny, or we can face this head-on. Yes, it's overwhelming. Yes, it's a massive problem. Yes, it's hard. Yes, it's scary. But it's time we examine, name our demons, lament, confess, and repent.

This may be a hard swallow for many of us who are White, and we may feel the defenses going up. That's *normal*. This is especially normal in the practice of examen. We as the church have got to zoom the lens out in our practice of examen. We must courageously look in a mirror that gives us insight into a shared history of sin and a matrix of power, privilege, and participation in oppression.

I'll never forget the first time I went through my own journey of examining the storm in my heart.

"I don't know, Tiffany, I just don't see it," I said after Tiffany, my African American classmate, brought up the subject of racism in America. I went on, "I just feel like racism is a thing of the past,

I mean, we elected an African American president, after all. I just feel like we're beating a dead horse and keep bringing something up that doesn't exist anymore."

Tiffany's demeanor changed as she noticeably shut down and slumped in her chair. The professor took a deep breath, sensing the tension in the room. "I think it's time we take a break." What I said to Tiffany was the dumbest thing I have ever said, because I was dead wrong.

I later read a pivotal essay written in the 1980s, in which Peggy McIntosh wrote, "I was taught to see racism only in individual acts of meanness, not in invisible systems conferring dominance on my group."[6] At the time of my comment, I was unaware of the invisible systemic issues that exist in America today that all too often marginalize entire people groups.

Then I went through a section on racial issues in my theology class at Northern Seminary, and everything I ever believed about the nonexistence of racism in America was blown into shreds in a matter of weeks. Suddenly, I became aware of the devastating historical implications of whiteness in America. Every day as I sat in class, I looked in the mirror. I listened to painful stories from my African American classmates who have seen the impact of racism in America. I heard stories of racial profiling in the city of Chicago, stories of my classmates being aware of their race on a daily basis, and stories of classmates who often feared harassment. For my whole life, I had a bootstrap philosophy: I believed that if someone worked hard enough in the United States, they could have a fair advantage as everyone else.

That day, as I listened to my classmates pour their hearts out, I could bear it no more. I saw myself in the mirror, I saw the power that I held, I saw the privilege that I had, and I saw the history and systems I stood on and that I was both implicit and complicit.

Tiffany, who I had so rudely written off just two years before sat in the same classroom as I did. I quickly raised my hand with tears rolling down my face, "Excuse me, could I just share something?" The entire class turned to see my distraught face. "Two years ago, I so wrongly wrote Tiffany off in the middle of class and told her that I didn't see racism. Tiffany, I need to ask for your forgiveness. I am sorry, I could not have been more wrong."

I felt naked. I felt sick. I hated the words I had said just two years before this moment.

Tiffany got up from her chair, walked across the room toward me, pulled me from my chair and embraced me. "I forgive you, Tara Beth." Together we wept.[7]

That was the beginning of learning how to examine my participation in harmful systems. Of course, practicing examen goes further than just race. We can add to the list classism, neonationalism, sexism, ideologies, exceptionalism, and so much more. The point is this: *we the church must first be willing to look in the mirror.* My concern is, whenever any *ism* comes up, so do our defenses. "I'm *not* _____." But does this reaction truly seek heartfelt, honest, and open examination? Perhaps we need to first name that it is *hard*—that is to examine, name, and repent. In *Divided by Faith,* Michael Emerson notes the great difficulty that many White evangelicals in particular have in seeing, naming, repenting, and responding to systemic injustices.[8]

I know this can feel overwhelming. I've been there, and I still am on this difficult journey of dismantling the many *isms* in my life. Pastorally, I want to tell you to not go on this journey alone.

The following are some things you can begin doing now to enter into the journey of examining the storm in your heart:

- Begin praying that the Lord would help you to see the storm in your heart.
- Ask God to break your heart for the things that break God's heart.
- Pray for empathy.
- Do as much of your own research as possible. Often, people of color are exhausted being the ones teaching the White church.
- Invite a group of trusted friends that will encourage you to press in, change, confess, and grow. A book club can be a safe space to wrestle through some of your toughest questions.
- If all else fails, close your mouth and simply listen.

If we, the people of God, can't even stand before Jesus and courageously pray, "Lord, search my heart," then are we truly bringing our full selves before God? I want to say this to my brothers and sisters in Christ: Have you examined any *isms* in your life? Or do you instead become defensive and angry? Have you asked God to search your heart when it comes to your participation in harmful systems?

My next question will take us to the next *practice* I'd like to address: Have you listened to people who are *not like you*?

PRACTICE LISTENING

Many Christians have seemingly abandoned a core theological truth that all are created in the image of God. Mae Elise Cannon and others note, "A healthy Christian understanding of the image of God should result in a deeper sense of unity that moves beyond human division. Instead, a distortion of that doctrine furthers division and hostility."[9] Within the churches I have pastored, there is often a thread of otherness, exclusion, and polarization. Although we are all created in the image of God, we have constructed various *isms* that keep us further and further. Again, the authors of *Forgive Us* write, "That shared story of being made in the image of God should yield a sense of human unity. The diseased imagination has allowed for the dysfunctional belief that one people group holds a higher standing before God than another people group."[10] Various systems and wounds divide us from one another, and not only have we abandoned the theological truth that all are created in God's image, but we have also failed to listen to and be in relationship with one another. Paul Borthwick says,

> "Homogeneous units" may accurately describe our congregational groupings. We instinctively prefer to be with people who are "just like us" in culture and appearance. But is this what God wants? Did Jesus die to "destroy the barrier, the dividing wall of hostility" and create "one new humanity" out of diverse peoples that we would stay separated from each other on this side of heaven (Eph 2:14-15)?[11]

We like to listen to those who look like us, worship like us, believe like us, and vote like us. Many choose to read those they will agree with, listen to news sources who will further cement their ideology or partisan politics, and embrace a theology they have believed their entire lives. In other words, we are *really good* at listening to those who affirm our *belief kingdom* we've spent a lifetime building. No wonder we are so polarized. It's nearly impossible for us to believe that those who don't embrace our belief kingdom are actually created in God's image—at least we treat them as if they aren't. Perhaps we are afraid of losing our positions of privilege and authority if we find out the kingdoms we have built aren't what we thought.

Imagine for a moment that we turned an ear to those with a different story. Imagine we see them as co–image bearers, sisters, or relatives. Imagine we spend time with them, learning to love and seeking to understand others who have altogether different belief systems, upbringings, cultures, ethnic identities, or socioeconomic statuses. Perhaps if we did this—in the name of love and *God's kingdom*—it would be *disarming*. Kim Thomas, a vice president for one of the nation's largest hospital systems and a lay leader at her church shares her story of being disarmed by a coworker's story:

> I am embarrassed to say that for forty years I didn't think we had a race issue in America. Several years ago, I began to slowly wake up from the coma I had been in. The coma that says, "Pull yourself up by your bootstraps," "I see no race," and "All Lives Matter." I started researching, and what I learned about oppression of the Black community in America was hard to stomach. It was gut-wrenching, and yet I know, as a White woman, I can never possibly fully comprehend racism. I can learn, I can seek to understand, but most importantly I can listen.
>
> The Instagrammed murder of George Floyd at the hands of a White police officer in Minneapolis had broad impacts. Social media was lit up with condemnation for the officer, and while the state of Minnesota seemingly dragged their feet on a murder charge, unrest grew. How long would this have to go on? I saw my Black friends posting on social

media a fear that I don't understand. One said, "If you ask me what my greatest fear is, I fear for my son every day. I pray for him every day, literally all day. It doesn't matter if he is smart, hardworking, kind, loving, thoughtful, respectful. He is seen as black, and he is seen as a threat." My heart is grieved, but even that is said from a place of privilege, White people can't walk in the shoes of people of color. We can stand alongside, we can appropriately speak out, but we don't understand and we can't speak for them.

George Floyd's murder came on the cusp of the COVID-19 pandemic. For three months, the world had mostly been on stay-at-home orders, and as protests began to be held nationwide I began to worry about the impacts of COVID-19 on the Black community. I work in health care and when my Black colleague and friend posted his same concerns, I began responding to his Facebook post when I realized reaching out directly was a better path. I began my message with the words "I am careful to speak into this because I don't know the answer." Often, when White people approach situations of race, we come in as know-it-alls rather than taking the posture of listening. As my colleague and I discussed the potential dangers of COVID-19 to the protesters, he began sharing his story of growing up as a Black man in South Los Angeles. Casually he mentioned how he had been cuffed and beaten by cops growing up. Then he mentioned how on a trip to visit his extended family he watched as cops beat his cousin unconscious while they hurled racial slurs at both of them.

I wept, and as our conversation wrapped up I realized how little I had known about him before that day. We worked side by side but in various roles for nineteen years: he had been my boss, my peer, my friend, my customer, and my colleague. We had countless conversations about our families, his grandchildren, hobbies, and work strategies. When I was moving my office last year, I pulled a card from him off the shelf: "We are here for you." He sent it with flowers when I had a miscarriage in 2004. And yet I didn't know his story. I didn't know and I will never comprehend the pain he has endured simply because he is a Black man in the United States of America.[12]

Through open and active listening, Kim was disarmed and began to see and understand a world she previously could not understand. She began to understand that just because she couldn't see racism every day, it didn't mean that it didn't exist. As I have learned to listen to my sisters and brothers of color, it is undeniable that their experience as people of color in America is different from my own.

Many want to know what to do about racism, and perhaps the most important place to start is with the simple act of listening. What is needed most during times of high racial tensions is a greater capacity for listening and making space for people of color. Tips for listening that seek to understand the stories of people of color include

- reading memoirs and books by people of color
- listening to podcasts from people of color
- finding White allies to help us better understand; people of color are exhausted by being the only ones teaching about racism
- attending a church in a neighborhood different from ours

- not making assumptions that every person of color has the same experience
- attending an activist rally or prayer vigil in our community during times when racial tensions are high
- seeking to understand what's below the surface of the other person's experience
- serving in our community alongside people of different ethnicities

Perhaps if we learned to listen, love, and understand one another, dividing walls of hostility would crumble. As it crumbles, we will discover that we are all invited to God's banquet table.

THE PRACTICE OF EATING

Many cities in America are becoming increasingly diverse due to the influx of refugees, immigration, and globalization. While this shift is a beautiful opportunity for the church to embrace a more diverse vision of the kingdom of God, it seems we've embraced a worldly vision of hostility, dividing walls, and boundary markers. We prefer to draw lines in the sand between us and them, and *them* refers to those who don't look, act, vote, shop, dress, and worship like us. An us-and-them mentality is considered by psychologists to be "othering." To "other" someone is to place them—whether an individual or people group—in a category that creates negative emotions.[13] Wendy Jones writes this about othering:

> Psychology has yielded some fairly grim news about othering, about the ease with which we view people as part of an out group and have negative emotions about them. Expose someone to an image of another person for fifty milliseconds (not enough time for conscious processing),

and the viewer's amygdala, a brain area involved in fear and aggression, will activate for other races/ethnicities. The fusiform face area, involved in facial recognition, will activate only for those of their own kind.[14]

The art of othering is an art Christians have become particularly good at doing. When we embrace the worldly art of othering, we produce acts of the *flesh* such as discord, bitterness, contempt, hatred, distrust, and aggression. We tend to be more hospitable, welcoming, and loving to people "of our kind," but Scripture calls us to extend love and hospitality to people of *all kinds*. We've discussed the importance of Christians examining the storm in our hearts and practicing deep listening that seeks to understand our sisters and brothers of color. Now let's consider how we might develop relationships consistent with the kingdom vision rooted in Scripture through the practice of table fellowship.[15]

Eating together is incredibly important to my family. It is a time when we recount the day's highs and lows to one another, and some of our best memories are made around the table. Several years ago, when we were eating, we were trying to explain to our four-year-old, Noah, that he needed to eat his broccoli so he could grow big and strong. After dinner, Noah began walking through the house attempting to pick up large pieces of furniture. As he would attempt to lift, he would grunt and huff with veins popping out on his neck and his face turning red. Eventually, he gave up, fell to the floor, and started to weep, "It's not working! You told me that if I eat my broccoli, I'd grow big and strong, but I can't pick up any of the furniture in the house!" We as a family laughed and laughed, and it's still one of our many favorite dinnertime memories.

Sacred moments and memories are made around the table. I first realized I was in love with Jeff when I was eating dinner with

Jeff. We announced our pregnancies to our family around the dinner table. The table is a special place. It was also a sacred place for Jesus.

THE TABLE FELLOWSHIP OF JESUS

Many have said that Jesus ate his way through the Gospels. Many of the stories couched within the Gospels are of Jesus eating at a table. Banquets, feasts, and other meals provide a significant backdrop for the ministry of Jesus. Not only that, but Jesus told a number of parables that included banquets and feasts. Jesus models an important practice for Christians during turbulent times, and while at a table he models his vision for the kingdom of God. Jesus' table practice is important because of *who* he ate with. In his book *Jesus and the Victory of God*, N. T. Wright writes, "He ate with sinners and kept company with people normally on or beyond the borders of respectable society."[16] Jesus not only tore down dividing walls of hostility at the cross but also in his life and ministry, including who he broke bread with.

There were many rules and regulations when it came to eating, and Jesus broke many of the social codes and boundaries. In Jewish literature much was written about who was acceptable for a Jew to eat with: "Separate yourself from the gentiles, and do not eat with them, and do not perform deeds like theirs. And do not become associates of theirs, because their deeds are defiled and all of their ways are contaminated, and despicable, and abominable."[17] All Jewish teachers knew these rules, and they would especially know that it was not acceptable to meet with anyone outside the boundary markers. But Jesus did exactly that.

Jesus broke all the ceremonial codes by extending and expanding table fellowship and eating with the "other." Let's look at one example found in Mark's Gospel:

> While Jesus was having dinner in Levi's house, many tax collectors and sinners were also sitting were eating with him and his disciples, for there were many who followed him. When the teachers of the law who were Pharisees saw him eating with the sinners and tax collectors, they asked his disciples: "Why does he eat with tax collectors and sinners?"
>
> On hearing this, Jesus said to them, "It is not the healthy who need a doctor, but the sick. I have not come to call the righteous, but sinners." (Mk 2:15-17)

It's likely that Levi, the former tax collector turned disciple, wanted to introduce his friends to the one who transformed his own life. Without pause, remorse, or reservations, Jesus graces a dinner party with "them." For the Jewish people, someone like Levi and his friends were "others." Jesus' dining with the tax collectors and sinners makes a statement to the many religious leaders looking on. Jesus didn't accidentally show up to this party but intentionally dines to extend brotherhood, acceptance, and hospitality. By sharing life with the socially unacceptable, Jesus is extending the kingdom table. Jesus extended social boundaries as an inclusive, hospitable, healing, and welcoming force. By eating with all the "wrong people," Jesus crossed boundaries and modeled a new and transformative vision of God's kingdom.

At the table Jesus practices love, listens, and shows mercy and grace. At the table Jesus models forgiveness, shows us the way of reconciliation, and gives us a glimpse into the future. At the table Jesus rejects an us-versus-them mentality, gives up status and pecking orders, stoops down and shows the way of downward service and sacrifice, and gives up the seat of privilege. At the table others were honored, social boundaries obliterated, power and privilege shared, and the voice of the invisible elevated. At the table others became brothers, foes became friends, and "those people" became family.

Practicing the table manners of Jesus is transformative for our own hearts and minds. At the table we not only share food with others, but we learn to share life. At the table we learn to understand those we may not understand. At the table we learn to celebrate unity, but not uniformity. At the table we learn to slow down and celebrate the stories of another. At the table we learn to practice hospitality. At the table we let go of status, privilege, and social boundaries.

Practicing the table manners of Jesus has been a significant part of my family's ministry. Jeff and I open our home almost weekly and sometimes twice weekly. When we first begin dinner, there may be a nervous or uncomfortable silence. Sometimes we worry we may run out of questions to ask and have nothing to talk about. However, something sacred *always* happens. As we begin eating, the conversation begins to roll, and often, before we know it, several hours have passed. I am delighted when everyone around the table is stuffed to the max, leaning back in their chairs, and sharing both laughter and heartfelt stories. At the table strangers become family. Grace Ji-Sun Kim and Graham Hill observe:

> Hospitality makes us fuller, richer, more Christlike people. We welcome people into our homes and lives and lands in anticipation of the home and age to come. In doing so we are a foretaste of our ultimate home and age to come in

Christ Jesus. The Spirit of hospitality opens our hearts to others, enables us to relish diversity, and inspires us to embrace the other.[18]

Hospitality and eating together, however, is not only about inviting others into our homes, where we control the environment and agenda. Eating together includes embracing the environments of others. Several years ago a coworker and I weren't seeing eye to eye. She is a Latina, and I was a stubborn White woman with many blind spots. I realized that she and I were going to continue to clash, so I asked her if we could start eating together. When our first lunch date came, I was quick to control the environment and suggested a standard restaurant in town. Thankfully, she was so loving and pastoral at that moment and said, "Actually, I'd like to take you to some small local restaurants owned by people of color when we eat together." We went, and it was such a gift for me to be in an environment she knew, loved, and had roots. There, she shared her family's story of immigration, she told me about the authentic Guatemalan food we shared, and she shared her heart. At the table we began to see one another as colaborers in Christ, sisters, and friends. Extending hospitality isn't about controlling the environment or welcoming people into my world; it's entering into the world of another with love, grace, and openness.

NAVIGATING THE STORM EMBOLDENED
BY THE SPIRIT OF LOVE

There is a storm at sea and within the church. Times are turbulent, and more than ever, it's time we take on practices to help us navigate the storm and partner with God in calming the storm. This begins with us, dear church. This storm will not be calmed with hard hearts, deaf ears, and small tables. Instead, we need Christians to be emboldened by the Spirit of love, hospitality, and mercy. We need the church to open its heart and ask God to show us the logs in our eyes. Come, dear church, let's embrace practices that will calm the storm. Examining the storms in our heart, listening to one another, and eating together are practices that must be reclaimed for a new day.

QUESTIONS FOR INDIVIDUALS AND GROUPS

1. The author believes we are in turbulent times. In what ways have you observed this turbulence in the church?

2. What kinds of practices have sustained you during turbulent times?

3. Do you agree or disagree that a major "storm" within the hearts of many Christians is racism? Why or why not?

4. How does the practice of examen help us see things about ourselves that we had not formerly known about ourselves?

5. If Christians refuse to take responsibility for their participation in systems that marginalize and harm entire people groups, what might be the consequences?

6. How do the table manners of Jesus define the kingdom of God?

7. What are practical ways we can embody the way of Jesus through eating together?

9

THE RADIANT FUTURE

I RECENTLY HEARD THAT THE AVERAGE ADULT spends 12 percent of the day thinking about the future, roughly one of every eight hours. Humans have the capability to imagine events in the future, while no other living creature can. Thinking about the future, dreaming about the future, and hoping for a certain kind of future is an incredible gift that we should not take for granted.

I would venture to say that if the average adult spends 12 percent of the day thinking about the future, then I easily spend 30 percent of the day thinking about the future. I am a dreamer, and when it comes to the church in North America, I have many hopes and dreams.

When I pastored a 115-year-old church, I would think about its future. I recognized that I stood on the shoulders of those who cared for the future generations by stewarding their resources well. I often asked, "What kind of church will we leave our children or grandchildren or nieces or nephews?" The decisions we make today (or our obedience or disobedience) will have ripple effects for generations to come.

Sometimes I think our imaginations are anemic, small, and worldly. Sure, we desire success, but is it the success of the kingdom or something else? We can believe in Jesus, attend worship every Sunday, and still have imaginations shaped more by this world than by Jesus.

Jesus spent a lot of time painting a vision for the church of the future. He talked about his relationship with the church, the ethics of the church, and the ways the church should engage with those who are hard to love.

I often wonder whether we are the church Jesus envisioned we'd be. Are we the church of the future that Jesus taught? Are we living into his dreams and revelations? Are we carrying the torch the disciples carried? I believe Jesus has a few things to teach us about the church of the future.

THE CHURCH OF THE FUTURE LIVES
OUT OF THE ABUNDANCE OF GOD

In the Gospel of John, as the cross was looming, we see Jesus' longing for the future church in this prayer:

> My prayer is not for [the disciples] alone. I pray also for those who will believe in me through their message, that all of them may be one, Father, just as you are in me and I am in you. May they also be in us so that the world may believe that you have sent me. I have given them the glory that you gave me, that they may be one as we are one—I in them and you in me—so that they may be brought to complete unity. Then the world will know that you sent me and have loved them even as you have loved me. (Jn 17:20-23)

Forty days after his death, the resurrected Jesus appeared to the disciples and both his heart for the church and his own nature are revealed in his many teachings. In one of Jesus' final conversations with Peter, he invites Peter to turn his eyes toward the future vision of the church.

Afterward Jesus appeared again to his disciples, by the Sea of Galilee. It happened this way: Simon Peter, Thomas (also known as Didymus), Nathanael from Cana in Galilee, the sons of Zebedee, and two other disciples were together. "I'm going out to fish," Simon Peter told them, and they said, "We'll go with you." So they went out and got into the boat, but that night they caught nothing.

Early in the morning, Jesus stood on the shore, but the disciples did not realize that it was Jesus.

He called out to them, "Friends, haven't you any fish?"

"No," they answered.

He said, "Throw your net on the right side of the boat and you will find some." When they did, they were unable to haul the net in because of the large number of fish.

Then the disciple whom Jesus loved said to Peter, "It is the Lord!" As soon as Simon Peter heard him say, "It is the Lord," he wrapped his outer garment around him (for he had taken it off) and jumped into the water. The other disciples followed in the boat, towing the net full of fish, for they were not far from shore, about a hundred yards. When they landed, they saw a fire of burning coals there with fish on it, and some bread.

Jesus said to them, "Bring some of the fish you have just caught." So Simon Peter climbed back into the boat and dragged the net ashore. It was full of large fish, 153, but even with so many the net was not torn. Jesus said to them, "Come and have breakfast." None of the disciples dared ask him, "Who are you?" They knew it was the Lord. Jesus came, took the bread and gave it to them, and did the same with the fish. This was now the third time Jesus appeared to his disciples after he was raised from the dead. (Jn 21:1-14)

Right away, we hear echoes of the signs and wonders Jesus performed in John's Gospel, including the miracle in Cana when Jesus turned water into wine, and the feeding of the masses. In both of these cases the *abundance of God* was highlighted. At the wedding at Cana, there was more wine than they knew what to do with. In the feeding of the masses, there was an abundance of fish and bread.

Here, when he sees the abundance of fish, John calls out, "It is the Lord!" He recognized the Lord in the abundant generosity of fish. In the following meal, Jesus is revealed as the giver of good gifts and life-sustaining nourishment.[1]

Scholar Gail O'Day makes an important observation about this text and John's Gospel. Over and over, Jesus emphasizes the future of the faith community through his teachings and the signs and wonders he performs. She notes that John 13–17 are devoted to the future of the church, and again this is revealed in John 17 as Jesus prays for the future faith community.[2]

Now the disciples (and readers) may wonder: *What will it be like after Jesus ascends to the Father? What are our lives supposed to be like? What about persecution? Will Jesus be with us?*

God's provision of the fish is an echo of the feeding of the masses. Gail O'Day says, "The vast quantity of fish in the disciples' net and the gracious meal of bread and fish show that God's gift is available in the risen Jesus just as it was in the incarnate Jesus."[3]

She notes that just as Jesus' ministry was inaugurated with a miracle of unprecedented abundance (Jn 2:1-11) so is the church's ministry. This story, then, reveals God's abundance for the postresurrection community. The church can trust and believe in God's abundance.

I hope you caught that and let it soak in. God's postresurrection abundance is available today. We can trust in the abundance of God. God's gifts are freely available to us so that we might steward them well and be propelled to radiance for the sake of the world and glory of God. We have been given

- Abundant blessings: "God is able to bless you abundantly, so that in all things at all times, having all that you need, you will abound in every good work" (2 Cor 9:8).

- Abundant power: "Now to him who is able to do immeasurably more than all we ask or imagine, according to his power that is at work within us" (Eph 3:20).

- Abundant life: "The thief comes only to steal and kill and destroy; I have come that they may have life, and have it to the full" (Jn 10:10).

- Abundant hope: "May the God of hope fill you with all joy and peace as you trust in him, so that you may overflow with hope by the power of the Holy Spirit" (Rom 15:13).

- Abundant wisdom: "If any of you lacks wisdom, you should ask God, who gives generously to all without finding fault, and it will be given to you" (Jas 1:5).

- Abundant love: "Hope does not put us to shame, because God's love has been poured out into our hearts through the Holy Spirit, who has been given to us" (Rom 5:5).

I could go on! We also have been given

- Abundant relationships
- Abundant goodness
- Abundant peace
- Abundant joy
- Abundant goodness
- Abundant patience
- Abundant presence

God is a God of abundance and goodness. As the disciples are likely anxious about what life will be like postresurrection, Jesus reminds them that abundance continues.

Life after the resurrection would not be bare bones. If anything, the power they witnessed through the signs and wonders of Jesus would now be made available to them in ways they had never known. The promised Holy Spirit would soon come upon them, and as Jesus promised, they would do greater things:

> Very truly I tell you, whoever believes in me will do the works I have been doing, and they will do even greater things than these, because I am going to the Father. And I will do whatever you ask in my name, so that the Father may be glorified in the Son. You may ask me for anything in my name, and I will do it. (Jn 14:12-14)

Jesus believed in the disciples, not because of their own abilities but because the abundance of God was made available to them and the future church.

Dear church, it may seem that these days are disorienting. Power is shifting, the status quo seems to be crumbling, success has been flipped on its head, and we're learning that perhaps the good ol' days had some serious problems. As things around us appear to be rapidly changing, it's easy for panic to set in.

But while much is changing, so much more has not changed. The unchanging goodness of God overflows and is made available to us today. The church can thrive in the abundant power and blessings of God. As the people of God *in Christ*, we need not fear the future—the gates of hell will not prevail.

THE CHURCH OF THE FUTURE
LOVES WITHOUT BORDERS

Jesus continues to reveal his heart for the church of the future with his conversation with Peter.

> When they had finished eating, Jesus said to Simon Peter, "Simon son of John, do you love me more than these?"
>
> "Yes, Lord," he said, "you know that I love you."
>
> Jesus said, "Feed my lambs."
>
> Again Jesus said, "Simon son of John, do you love me?"
>
> He answered, "Yes, Lord, you know that I love you."
>
> Jesus said, "Take care of my sheep."
>
> The third time he said to him, "Simon son of John, do you love me?"
>
> Peter was hurt because Jesus asked him the third time, "Do you love me?" He said, "Lord, you know all things; you know that I love you."
>
> Jesus said, "Feed my sheep. Very truly I tell you, when you were younger you dressed yourself and went where you wanted; but when you are old you will stretch out your hands, and someone else will dress you and lead you where you do not want to go." Jesus said this to indicate the kind of death by which Peter would glorify God. Then he said to him, "Follow me!"
>
> Peter turned and saw that the disciple whom Jesus loved was following them. (This was the one who had leaned back

against Jesus at the supper and had said, "Lord, who is going to betray you?") When Peter saw him, he asked, "Lord, what about him?"

Jesus answered, "If I want him to remain alive until I return, what is that to you? You must follow me." Because of this, the rumor spread among the believers that this disciple would not die. But Jesus did not say that he would not die; he only said, "If I want him to remain alive until I return, what is that to you?"

This is the disciple who testifies to these things and who wrote them down. We know that his testimony is true.

Jesus did many other things as well. If every one of them were written down, I suppose that even the whole world would not have room for the books that would be written. (Jn 21:15-25)

Imagine Peter's anxiety. He's denied the Lord three times. What was Jesus going to say to him? Would he shame him? Cut him loose?

But instead Jesus begins to ask Peter a series of questions, "Peter, do you love me?" Jesus asks three times. And every time Peter answers, Jesus asks him to feed his sheep. Just as Jesus has laid down his life for the sheep, now Jesus is asking Peter to do the same—love one another. Furthermore, many scholars note that these three questions are Peter's reinstatement. But as Jesus has made his love known, so he wants Peter to do the same. Jesus is calling Peter to live a life of love that matches Jesus' love by both caring for the sheep and laying down his life. Every time Peter answers, he is pledging his allegiance to do this, and he is declaring that there are no limits on his love.

Jesus is calling Peter to love abundantly as Jesus has loved abundantly. Jesus' call to Peter to feed Jesus' sheep is God's call for Peter to share the gift of abundance.

This, no doubt, scared Peter. It seemed so extreme; perhaps too abundant. Too much. Too far. I imagine Peter's heart pounding and his mind racing. "But what about John? Will he have to go to this extreme? Will he have to lay down his life?" he wonders.

Except Jesus calls Peter to lay down his life, not John. It's as if Jesus is encouraging Peter: "Don't worry, keep your eyes on me, and look to me for the abundant life, nothing else. Peter, don't worry about others. Keep your eyes on me. Yes, you're called to live a life of suffering, trials, and difficulty; that much is true, but keep your eyes on me."

Let's hit the pause button on that for a moment. Did you read what Jesus was calling Peter to?

- Suffering
- Trials
- Difficulty
- Laying down his life

Where I come from, those words are often linked to *failure, not success*. When there is suffering, something must be wrong, not right. When there are trials, we must have made a wrong turn. When there is extreme difficulty, it's likely we are failing, not succeeding. And yet this is one of Jesus' vision-casting speeches to Peter before ascending to the Father. Can you imagine a football coach giving his team this kind of speech before the biggest games of their lives? Perhaps it's time that we—the predominately White evangelical church—lay some things down. Before rebirth, revival, and renewal comes difficulty and death. Consider what we might need to lay down at the altar of success:

- control
- power

- individuality
- the limelight
- comfort

STEWARDING THE ABUNDANCE FOR LOVE

So it is for the church of the future; how far will people of the resurrection be willing to go? What kind of limits will we place on loving Jesus? Jesus calls the disciples, people of the resurrection, and the church of the future to live lives shaped by the love of Jesus. That is, to love abundantly without limits and without borders.

What's remarkable about the John 21 passage is something that is profoundly overlooked. Let's just reframe this with the word we like to use in America, *success*. This passage is radically different and says nothing of the sort. The resurrection community is marked by the self-sacrificial and abundant love of Jesus.

While many today wouldn't call suffering and death successful, the metric by which Jesus measures the church is different. We want growth, money, and bigger buildings, all the bells and whistles, but Jesus desires our love and faithfulness. Love is an indicator of faithfulness—that is, a people shaped and marked by the abundant love of Jesus is the vision for the Christian life, not worldly success.

We are not marked by our failures, weaknesses, politics, the millennials we attract, our cool music is, or our awesome website; rather, Jesus wants our self-sacrificial, boundary-breaking, indiscriminate love.

The question for us is, Are we who Jesus has called us to be? Hear again the words of Jesus to Peter, but now addressed to us: "Do you love me more than these?" Does Jesus have our loyalty? Allegiance? Faithfulness? Love?

THE CHURCH OF THE FUTURE LIVES BOLDLY

It was October 2005, and some of the last items were unloaded from the mid-size U-Haul and placed in my new home in rural upstate New York. I was twenty-three, fresh out of college, and about to start my first job as an associate pastor at a lovely Nazarene church. As a flatlander, Midwestern girl, I was enamored with the foothills of upstate New York. It was a dream to live in such a lovely place, and I was ready to take on the world, except I wasn't sure if I really was ready.

Bourbonnais, Illinois, was the only hometown I had ever known. While I was privileged to travel the world in my teens and twenties, the only zip code I called home was 60914. My parents were always either in the next room or even just two miles away from my college campus. When my dad first drove me to Olivet Nazarene University, he cried the entire two-mile drive; and now I watched Dad cry nearly thirteen hours in a U-Haul from Bourbonnais to Owego, New York.

For the first time in my adult life, I had to imagine a future without my parents just around the corner. It seemed almost fitting that it was a dreary, cold, rainy October afternoon as I watched my parents pull away from the old parsonage, sitting on the side of a foothill. I looked around this new home with barely any furniture, fell to the floor, and wept on top of that musty, old, pink carpet. I was overwhelmingly grief-stricken. It was so hard for me to imagine a future without my parents in the next room or down the street. What kind of adult would I be without my now-distant parents? Would I have enough courage and boldness to live this new chapter of my life?

I often wonder what kind of grief the disciples must have felt as they watched Jesus ascend to the throne. I would imagine that for the forty days the risen Jesus appeared to the disciples, the disciples likely grew rather comfortable and maybe even dependent with Jesus around. And yet, over this forty-day period, Jesus was preparing them to live *without* his earthly presence.

As Jesus prepared them through teachings, signs, and wonders, he spoke to them as if he believed in them. He warned them that it would be strenuous, hard, and costly. And yet he commissioned them to an audacious task: "You will receive power when the Holy Spirit comes on you; and you will be my witnesses in Jerusalem, and in all Judea and Samaria, and to the ends of the earth" (Acts 1:8).

In this commission, Jesus is opening their minds to their participation in God's redemptive reality, not only for Israel but the entire earth. Connecting this to the Spirit's outpouring, Jesus informs them that they would be participants in this redemptive work. They were commissioned to participate in healing, driving out demons, proclaiming the good news. In the power of the Spirit, they would pursue the captive, the prisoner, the poor, the broken, the sick, the widow, the orphan, the outcast, the distracted, the brokenhearted, and the lame. And in pursuing them, they would point to a reality much bigger than themselves; that is, Jesus is alive, the truth, the healer, the redeemer, the deliverer, and the light of the world. And in the power of the Holy Spirit, they would declare this to a weary world, desperate for answers.

They were given a mission. And then, just like that, Jesus ascended to the throne as the bewildered disciples watched. Were they wondering what life would be like without Jesus on earth? They could hardly comprehend Jesus' promise of his presence in the gift of the Holy Spirit.

But as the book of Acts unfolds, we see this ragtag group of disciples was unstoppable. Without Jesus physically by their side, his seemingly impossible mission was lived out in the teachings, the preaching, the healings, the generosity, and the life of the early church. The mission given to them is no different from our mission today. Different context? Sure. Different idols? Definitely. A different mission? No.

And perhaps what is most mind-bending is that the challenges today are no more significant than they were then. If anything, so much more was at stake over two thousand years ago than perhaps today. Their work was profoundly dangerous. They were burned at the stake, ripped from their homes, thrown into prison, and stoned to death. And yet the early church took up this mantel with unstoppable force, boldness, and passion. They were a force to be reckoned with, even in the face of death.

The winds are howling and the ground is shaking in and around the church. It is, no doubt, hard, scary, and concerning. Not knowing what the future will look like is even more concerning. But we are gifts to steward through the storm the abundant gifts God has given us.

UNSTOPPABLE

Let's return to the scene of the disciples standing, mouths agape, watching Jesus ascend to the Father.

> After he said this, he was taken up before their very eyes, and a cloud hid him from their sight.
>
> They were looking intently up into the sky as he was going, when suddenly two men dressed in white stood beside them. "Men of Galilee," they said, "why do you stand here looking into the sky? This same Jesus, who has been

taken from you into heaven, will come back in the same way you have seen him go into heaven."

Daniel 7 includes a scene of powerful imagery that most science-fiction writers would consider to be gold. Daniel has a vision of four great beasts that come out of the sea and stand in a courtroom speaking with arrogance and boasting about power. These beasts represented the worldly, chaotic, and oppressive powers of the day, including Babylon, the Medes, Greece, and Persia. These beasts who brag of their power through killing and devastation represent wicked human empires of our world. In Daniel's vision, God presides in this courtroom:

> In my vision at night I looked, and there before me was one like a son of man, coming with the clouds of heaven. He approached the Ancient of Days and was led into his presence. He was given authority, glory and sovereign power; all nations and peoples of every language worshiped him. His dominion is an everlasting dominion that will not pass away, and his kingdom is one that will never be destroyed. (Dan 7:13-14)

The arrogant beasts were eventually silenced; God gives power, authority, and everlasting dominion to the Son of Man. Throughout various places in the Gospels, Jesus is the Son of Man. No doubt, when Jesus took his final breath and cried out, "It is finished," he believed that he would go to the tomb only to rise again, and soon the power of the beasts would be broken. Jesus would be victorious over the powers, arrogance, dominion, and darkness of these evil beasts.

Not only would Jesus be victorious, but a new kind of kingdom would be unleashed—it's an alternative way of living for a world held captive by the powers of the beast. In this new kind of kingdom, power would be flipped on its head, that is, empowerment instead of coercion, love instead of oppression, peace instead of violence, inclusion instead of exclusion, *shalom* instead of war, sacrificial, selfless love instead of selfishness.

While the beasts of this world seek to destroy, those who are in Christ will be victorious. Death, destruction, and destructive power will be no more, and those who die with Christ will be raised to new life.

Jesus knew the cross wouldn't be defeated. Jesus knew that the powers of evil would be left in the grave. And now, at last, as the disciples stand with mouths agape, Jesus is exalted to the highest place as King, Lord, and Prince of Peace. At his name every knee shall bow and tongue confess that "Jesus is Lord."

Why then was the early church such an *unstoppable force* even in the face of evil, oppression, violence, and arrogance? Why were they so bold? They knew the visions of Daniel 7 has been fulfilled. This Jewish rabbi born on the margins of Bethlehem, who rode donkeys, fished on boats, ate with all the "wrong people," healed the sick, and loved the sinner; this rabbi who the disciples left everything to follow; this rabbi who suffered on the cross, died, and was buried is now *King over all*. The worldly beast has been put to shame, and this Jewish rabbi is not only victorious but is King over all.

As we read through the book of Acts, the early church stared the arrogant beast in the face with unstoppable confidence and force. As Stephen was stoned to death (Acts 7), the evil beast was seen in the faces of those who hurled insults and stones. The beast was also seen in the faces of Nero and Domitian and the Roman Empire, who breathed hate, evil, arrogance, and mockery. And yet Stephen, Peter, Paul, John, and the early church were still a force to be reckoned with. They faced these monsters with confidence because they truly believed these beasts could not stop the fledgling church. They knew how the story would end. They knew that in Christ they had been given power and authority to disarm the beasts of this world, and they knew they had the key to a better way of living—*the way* of living.

Dear church, gather around for a moment. Lean in and lend an ear. I have something to say to all of us:

This is still the present reality.

Jesus is presently reigning as King.

This King is among us.

The beasts of this world do not get the last word in our lives.

Those who are in Christ are victorious.

Read those truths again. Allow those words to settle into your bones, your heart, and your mind. Read them and pray them until you know it to be true. Read it and pray it until an emboldened spirit rises up. What if we—the bride of Christ—lived today with this same unstoppable confidence? What if we—those who are in Christ—were a force to be reckoned with? What if we—the people of God—were emboldened in such a way that we not only stared the evil beasts in the face but lived in such a way that we offer an alternative way of living?

Dear church, listen up and lean in. While it may seem at times the evil beasts of this world are winning, the book of Revelation tells us that our story doesn't end that way. We have news to tell, dear ones. We have work to do. We are invited into a vision, a purpose, and a way of living that is much bigger than any worldly force.

EMBOLDENED TO DISMANTLE THE BEAST

Harriet Tubman, an emboldened woman, was born into slavery on a Maryland plantation in 1822.[4] She knew the face of the evil beast quite well. And yet she was a force to be reckoned with. Growing up, she saw family members treated harshly. Her mother read the Scriptures to her, and I imagine Harriet's mind was lit up with God's vision of a vibrant kingdom. As she heard the story of God, perhaps her heart raced as she heard of an alternative kingdom inaugurated in King Jesus.

At the age of twenty-six, Harriet escaped the grips of this worldly beast and decided to create an alternative path for others who were held captive by this beast. She risked her own life and was an unstoppable force as she led countless slaves to freedom on the Underground Railroad. She gave glory to the King, "'Twant me, 'twas the Lord. I always told him, 'I trusts to you. I don't know where to go or what to do, but I expect you to lead me,' and he always did." Abolitionist Thomas Garrett said, "I never met with any person of any color who had more confidence in the voice of God, as spoken direct to her soul."[5]

We are living in the middle of a shift and an uprising within the church. We as the people of God can point fingers away from ourselves or we can deny; or we can take this head-on and embrace the radiance of Christ. I believe in my bones that this is a moment for us as God's people. This shifting and shaking don't have to break us; it can instead create room for new life. But are we willing to do the hard things? Are we willing to not only face the beastly powers of this world but dismantle and disarm them? Are we willing to untangle ourselves from the grip the beast has on us? Are we willing to speak prophetically to the powers of the beast, and are we willing to lament the ways we've become entangled with the beast?

We are called to live as an emboldened and *radiant* people of God in a weary world. We are emboldened not by our own power, but out of the abundance of God. May we be a people who steward the gifts of God so we can radiate God's love to the world.

May we live emboldened, empowered, and ready—as though we know this to be true. May we be the church of the future Jesus envisioned, died for, and rose for. May we be the church of the future that the early church believed we would be.

> God, whose purpose is to kindle,
> now ignite us with your fire.
> While the earth awaits your burning,
> with your passion us inspire.
> Overcome our sinful calmness,
> stir us with your saving name.
> Baptize with your fiery Spirit,
> crown our lives with tongues of flame.
> God, who still a sword delivers
> rather than a placid peace,
> with your sharpened word disturb us,
> from complacency release!
> Save us now from satisfaction,
> when we privately are free,
> yet are undisturbed in spirit
> by our neighbor's misery.
> God, who in your holy gospel
> wills that all should truly live,
> make us sense our share of failure,
> our tranquillity forgive.
> Teach us courage as we struggle
> in all liberating strife.
> Lift the smallness of our vision
> by your own abundant life.[6]

QUESTIONS FOR INDIVIDUALS AND GROUPS

1. How often do you think about the future? When you think about the future, what do you often think about?

2. Think about the church in twenty years. What do you hope for?

3. In what ways has our imagination for the church been "anemic"?

4. What kind of church do you believe Jesus believes we can be?

5. How would we look different if we became the church Jesus believes we can be?

6. The early church was an unstoppable force in the face of adversity. What would it look like for the church of today to lean into the instincts of the early church?

7. After reading this book, describe a "radiant" church. Spend time in prayer that we can be the radiant church you hope for and the radiant church Jesus believes we can be.

ACKNOWLEDGMENTS

It has been said that writing a book is a lot like birthing a baby. As a mother of two, I can attest that the parallels are stunning. Birthing this book has been a daunting and vulnerable work of love, and I could have never done it without the many midwives at my side.

First, to the love of my life, Jeff. For all the times you took the boys out for a fishing day so I could cram in a few hours of writing, and for all the times you listened to me cry about throwing this entire book out the window, thank you. You are patient, kind, generous, humble, and this book would have never happened without your cheerleading and love.

To my sweet baby boys, Caleb and Noah, thank you for your patience in waiting for me to make you lunch, to jump on the trampoline with you, or for going swimming while I write.

To Kim Thomas, the best friend I could ever ask for. Thank you for the many times you picked me up off the floor in this writing process. You are the one and true Olivia Pope, and thank you for helping me find creative writing spaces, for digging up encouragement for me, and for the constant push to keep going.

To the world's greatest therapist—my therapist—Dr. Laura Harbert. When I stopped believing I was a writer, when I stopped believing in my own voice, you reminded me over and over that I have a truth to declare, even when it's scary. Thank you for being "in this with me."

To Mom, Dad, Stu, and Lynn, thank you for the many times you cared for the children while I hid in a room to write. Jeff and I are fortunate to have you, and so are the boys. To my Home Group, thank you for the prayers, encouragement, and the gift of doing life together during this writing process.

Finally, to PazNaz, thank you for being the church to *me and my family*. Thank you for your radiance, love, humility, and bright witness in Pasadena. I was so grateful to be on this journey with you, and I will always love you.

NOTES

INTRODUCTION: A DIM LIGHT

[1]This and the following paragraph are adapted from Tara Beth Leach, "Embracing the Culture of the Kingdom of God," *The Foundry Community*, August 10, 2017, www.thefoundrycommunity.com/embracing-the-culture-of-the-kingdom -of-god.

[2]Lisa Sharon Harper, "Will Evangelicalism Surrender?" *Still Evangelical?* ed. Mark Labberton (Downers Grove, IL: InterVarsity Press, 2018), 30.

[3]Harper, "Will Evangelicalism Surrender?" 30.

1. THE CALL TO RADIANCE

[1]"Religion," *Gallup*, accessed July 13, 2020, https://news.gallup.com/poll/1690 /religion.aspx.

[2]David Kinnaman and Gabe Lyons, *UnChristian* (Grand Rapids: Baker, 2007), 26.

[3]David Fitch, *The End of Evangelicalism? Discerning a New Faithfulness for Mission: Towards an Evangelical Political Theology* (Eugene, OR: Cascade Books, 2011), 2.

[4]Rachel Held Evans, Twitter,@RachelHeldEvans, January 10, 2018, 12:27 p.m., https://twitter.com/rachelheldevans/status/951158906818121729?lang=en.

[5]Eugene Cho, *Thou Shalt Not Be a Jerk: A Christian's Guide to Engaging Politics* (Colorado Springs, CO: David C. Cook, 2020), 17.

[6]Scot McKnight, *The Sermon on the Mount* (Grand Rapids: Zondervan, 2013), 1.

[7]Soong-Chan Rah, *Prophetic Lament: A Call for Justice in Troubled Times* (Downers Grove, IL: InterVarsity Press, 2015), 23.

[8]Grace Ji-Sun Kim and Graham Hill, *Healing Our Broken Humanity: Practices for Revitalizing the Church and Renewing the World* (Downers Grove, IL: Inter-Varsity Press, 2018), 43.

2. THE RADIANT STORY

[1]Christena Cleveland, *Disunity in Christ* (Downers Grove, IL: InterVarsity Press, 2013), 33.

[2]Cleveland, *Disunity in Christ*, 34.

[3]John C. Nugent, *Endangered Gospel: How Fixing the World Is Killing the Gospel* (Eugene, OR: Cascade, 2016), 128.

[4]Nugent, *Endangered Gospel*, 128.

[5]For further reading see John Howard Yoder, *Christian Witness to the State* (St. Joseph, MI: Herald Press, 2007); Brian Zahnd, *Postcards from Babylon: The Church in America Exile* (London: Spello Press, 2019); Scot McKnight, *Kingdom Conspiracy* (Grand Rapids: Brazos, 2016).

[6]McKnight, *Kingdom Conspiracy*, 28.

[7]Eugene Cho, *Thou Shalt Not Be a Jerk: A Christian's Guide to Engaging Politics* (Colorado Springs, CO: David C. Cook, 2020), 109.

[8]Cho, *Thou Shalt Not Be a Jerk*, 109.

[9]Cho, *Thou Shalt Not Be a Jerk*, 110.

[10]Richard Rohr, "The Dualistic Mind," *The Center for Action and Contemplation News Letter* January 29, 2019, https://cac.org/the-dualistic-mind-2017-01-29.

[11]David Zahl, *Seculosity* (Minneapolis: Fortress Press, 2019), 96.

[12]Eugene H. Person, *The Pastor: A Memoir* (New York: HarperCollins, 2011), 143.

3. THE RADIANT VISION OF JESUS

[1]Greg Boyd, *Cross Vision* (Minneapolis: Fortress Press, 2017), 37.

[2]For even further reading see Greg Boyd, *The Crucifixion of the Warrior God*, vols. 1-2 (Minneapolis: Fortress Press, 2017).

[3]Boyd, *Cross Vision*, 36.

4. THE RADIANT KING AND KINGDOM

[1]Michael Gorman, *Becoming the Gospel: Paul, Participation, and Mission* (Grand Rapids: Eerdmans, 2015), 23.

[2]Scot McKnight, *The Sermon on the Mount*, Story of God Bible Commentary 21 (Grand Rapids: Zondervan, 2013), 1.

5. THE RADIANT WITNESS

[1] C. S. Lewis, *Mere Christianity* (New York: HarperCollins, 1952), 208.

[2] Michael Frost, *Surprise the World* (Colorado Springs, CO: NavPress, 2016), 7-8.

[3] Glen Stassen, *Sermon on the Mount* (San Francisco: Jossey-Bass, 2006), 58.

[4] Scot McKnight, *The Sermon on the Mount* (Grand Rapids: Zondervan, 2013), 45.

[5] Rodney Stark, *The Triumph of Christianity* (New York: HarperCollins, 2011), 112.

[6] Peter Kotz, "Peace Lutheran Staved Off Death by Taking 'Love Thy Neighbor' to a Radical Extreme," *City Pages*, October 23, 2019, www.citypages.com/news/peace-lutheran-staved-off-death-by-taking-love-thy-neighbor-to-a-radical-extreme/563648921.

[7] Kotz, "Peace Lutheran Staved Off Death."

6. THE RADIANT PARTNERSHIP

[1] Carolyn Custis James, *Malestrom* (Grand Rapids: Zondervan, 2015), 53.

[2] James, *Malestrom*, 51.

[3] James, *Malestrom*, 53.

[4] Scot McKnight, *The Blue Parakeet* (Grand Rapids: Zondervan, 2008), 216.

[5] McKnight, *Blue Parakeet*, 216.

[6] McKnight, *Blue Parakeet*, 206.

[7] Rebecca McLaughlin, *Confronting Christianity* (Wheaton, IL: Crossway, 2019), 136.

[8] Scot McKnight, *King Jesus Gospel* (Grand Rapids: Zondervan, 2016).

[9] The following paragraphs addressed to the author's "sisters" are lightly adapted from Tara Beth Leach, "Dear Woman in Ministry, You Are a Warrior and You Are also Clay," *Tara Beth Leach* (blog), June 12, 2018, https://tarabethleach.com/dear-woman-in-ministry-you-are-a-warrior-and-you-are-also-clay.

7. RADIANT EVANGELISM

[1] "Almost Half of Practicing Christian Millennials Say Evangelism Is Wrong," *Barna*, February 5, 2019, www.barna.com/research/millennials-oppose-evangelism.

[2] Noemi Vega Quiñones, "Go and Make Disciples. But First, Stop," *Christianity Today*, September 2019, 21.

[3] James Choung, *True Story: A Christianity Worth Believing In* (Downers Grove, IL: InterVarsity Press, 2009), 191.

[4] C. S. Lewis, *Mere Christianity* (New York: Simon & Schuster, 1996), 171.

[5] Lesslie Newbigin, *The Gospel in a Pluralist Society* (Grand Rapids: Eerdmans, 1989), 56.

[6] Michael Frost, *Surprise the World* (Colorado Springs, CO: NavPress, 2016), 75.

[7]David Fitch, *Faithful Presence: Seven Disciplines That Shape the Church for Mission*, (Downers Grove, IL: InterVarsity Press, 2016).

[8]Scot McKnight, *King Jesus Gospel* (Grand Rapids: Zondervan, 2016), 50.

[9]Michael Gorman uses the phrase "caught up" in reference to the apostle Paul and the early church being caught up in God's mission, God's character, and God's life. Michael Gorman, *Becoming the Gospel: Paul, Participation, and Mission* (Grand Rapids: Eerdmans, 2015).

[10]Gorman, *Becoming the Gospel*, 45.

8. RADIANT PRACTICES

[1]M. Eugene Boring, *Matthew-Mark*, ed. Leander Keck, New Interpreters Bible Commentary 8 (Nashville: Abingdon, 1995), 327.

[2]Sean Palmer, "Why Christians Are Incapable of Racial Healing," Missio Alliance, August 17, 2017, www.missioalliance.org/confession-evasion-christians-incapable-racial-healing.

[3]Richard Foster, *Prayer: Finding the Heart's True Home* (New York: HarperCollins, 1992), 29.

[4]See Dominique Gilliard, *Rethinking Incarceration: Advocating for Justice That Restores* (Downers Grove, IL: InterVarsity Press, 2018).

[5]Soong-Chan Rah, *Prophetic Lament* (Downers Grove, IL: InterVarsity Press, 2015), 185-86.

[6]Peggy McIntosh, "White Privilege: Unpacking the Invisible Knapsack," 1.

[7]The story of Tara Beth and Tiffany is adapted from post by Tara Beth Leach, "The Dumbest Thing I Ever Did Say," *Tara Beth Leach* (blog), May 7, 2014, http://tarabethleach.com/the-dumbest-thing-i-ever-did-say.

[8]Michael Emerson and Christian Smith, *Divided by Faith: Evangelical Religion and the Problem of Race in America* (Oxford: Oxford University Press, 2000).

[9]Mae Elise Cannon, Lisa Sharon Harper, Troy Jackson, and Soong-Chan Rah, *Forgive Us: Confessions of a Compromised Faith* (Grand Rapids: Zondervan, 2014), 171.

[10]Cannon et al., *Forgive Us*, 171.

[11]Paul Borthwick, *Western Christians in Global Missions: What's the Role of the North American Church?* (Downers Grove, IL: InterVarsity Press, 2012), 182-83.

[12]Kim Thomas, email communication written May 30, 2020 at 1:10 p.m., used with permission.

[13]Wendy Jones, "Us Versus Them, or Not Our Kind," *Psychology Today*, November 6, 2018. www.psychologytoday.com/us/blog/intersubjective/201811/us-versus-them-or-not-our-kind.

[14]Jones, "Us Versus Them, or Not Our Kind."

[15]I recognize that this chapter is not a comprehensive map for racial justice and is lacking many important steps and elements. This chapter touches the tip of the iceberg, and I encourage all readers to take a deeper dive into reconciliation, beginning with Brenda Salter McNeil, *Roadmap to Reconciliation: Moving Communities into Unity, Wholeness and Justice* (Downers Grove, IL: InterVarsity Press, 2015).

[16]N. T. Wright, *Jesus and the Victory of God* (Minneapolis: Fortress Press, 1992), 149.

[17]*Jubilees* 22:16, The Book of Jubilees in Apocrypha and Pseudepigrapha of the Old Testament.

[18]Grace Ji-Sun Kim and Graham Hill, *Healing Our Broken Humanity: Practices for Revitalizing the Church and Renewing the World* (Downers Grove, IL: InterVarsity Press, 2018), 121.

9. THE RADIANT FUTURE

[1]Gail O'Day, *John's Gospel*, New Interpreters Bible Commentary (Nashville: Abingdon Press, 1995), 852.

[2]O'Day, *John's Gospel*, 852.

[3]O'Day, *John's Gospel*, 852.

[4]Eric Metaxas, "Harriet Tubman, on the Money: Resisting Evil, Trusting God," *Christian Headlines*, May 6, 2016, www.christianheadlines.com/columnists /breakpoint/harriet-tubman-on-the-money-resisting-evil-trusting-god.html.

[5]Metaxas, "Harriet Tubman, on the Money."

[6]D. Elton Trueblood, "Thou, Whose Purpose Is to Kindle," c. 1956.

Missio Alliance

Missio Alliance has arisen in response to the shared voice of pastors and ministry leaders from across the landscape of North American Christianity for a new "space" of togetherness and reflection amid the issues and challenges facing the church in our day. We are united by a desire for a fresh expression of evangelical faith, one significantly informed by the global evangelical family. Lausanne's Cape Town Commitment, "A Confession of Faith and a Call to Action," provides an excellent guidepost for our ethos and aims.

Through partnerships with schools, denominational bodies, ministry organizations, and networks of churches and leaders, Missio Alliance addresses the most vital theological and cultural issues facing the North American church in God's mission today. We do this primarily by convening gatherings, curating resources, and catalyzing innovation in leadership formation.

Rooted in the core convictions of evangelical orthodoxy, the ministry of Missio Alliance is animated by a strong and distinctive theological identity that emphasizes

Comprehensive Mutuality: Advancing the partnered voice and leadership of women and men among the beautiful diversity of the body of Christ across the lines of race, culture, and theological heritage.

Hopeful Witness: Advancing a way of being the people of God in the world that reflects an unwavering and joyful hope in the lordship of Christ in the church and over all things.

Church in Mission: Advancing a vision of the local church in which our identity and the power of our testimony is found and expressed through our active participation in God's mission in the world.

In partnership with InterVarsity Press, we are pleased to offer a line of resources authored by a diverse range of theological practitioners. The resources in this series are selected based on the important way in which they address and embody these values, and thus, the unique contribution they offer in equipping Christian leaders for fuller and more faithful participation in God's mission.

missioalliance.org | twitter.com/missioalliance | facebook.com/missioalliance

More Titles from
InterVarsity Press and Missio Alliance

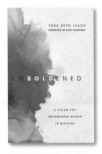

Emboldened
978-0-8308-4524-8

Faithful Presence
978-0-8308-4127-1

Redeeming Sex
978-0-8308-3639-0

**Rediscipling the
White Church**
978-0-8308-4597-2

**Seven Practices for the
Church on Mission**
978-0-8308-4142-4

Sojourner's Truth
978-0-8308-4552-1

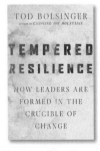

Tempered Resilience
978-0-8308-4164-6

Uncommon Church
978-0-8308-4162-2

White Awake
978-0-8308-4393-0

*For a list of IVP email newsletters, including information
about our latest ebook releases, please visit*
www.ivpress.com/eu1.